FEARS AND PHOBIAS

Overcoming Common Problems Series

Overcoming Common Problems Series

Overcoming Common Problems

FEARS AND PHOBIAS

Dr Tony Whitehead
M.B., B.S., M.R.C.Psych., D.P.M.

SHELDON PRESS
LONDON

First published in Great Britain in 1980 by
Sheldon Press, Marylebone Road, London NW1 4DU

Thanks are due to George Allen &
Unwin (Publishers) Ltd for permission
to reproduce the list of phobias in
Appendix 1 from *Phobias and Obsessions*
by Joy Melville.

Printed in Great Britain by
Fletcher & Son Ltd, Norwich

ISBN 0 85969 187 X

Contents

I

Introduction

Everyone knows something of fear and most of us have a phobia or two. Unfortunately, experiencing fear, becoming anxious and being abnormally afraid of an object, thing, or situation, does not bring with it understanding of these things within ourselves, or in others.

In this book an attempt will be made to examine fear, anxiety, and phobias in the hope of explaining them to a degree which will make them better understood and hence easier to deal with, and if necessary correct. Perhaps the most important point to make is that fear and anxiety are normal parts of human experience and even abnormal fears and anxieties are common to most of us. The individual who is terrified at even the thought of going into a confined space may look upon himself as abnormal, odd, and even in danger of going mad. Because of this he may be loath to talk to anyone about his fear, and so, keeping everything to himself the situation worsens, with the added anxiety of what it means and what it may foretell. Very many people have this fear of a confined space, described as claustrophobia, and the same applies to almost every example of abnormal fear. There are very few ideas, sensations, thoughts, or fears that are not common to many others.

This is a book mainly about phobias, so it is worth while examining the origin of the word and mentioning some famous phobics.

The word phobia was first used as a medical one by Celsus, a Roman creator of encyclopaedias, when he used the term hydrophobia. Celsus lived in the first century A.D., but morbid fears had been around long before he wrote his encyclopaedia. Rather oddly, mention of phobias by name only appeared in the literature of psychiatry in the nineteenth century. A very early description of a phobic condition, though the word was not used, is by Hippocrates. He described two victims of phobias. Describing the condition of someone called Nicanor, he wrote, 'When he used to begin drinking, the girl flute player would frighten him; as soon as he heard the first note of the flute at a banquet he would be beset by terror. He used to say he could scarcely contain himself when night fell but during the day he would hear the instrument without feeling any emotion. This lasted a long time with him.' He goes on to describe Damocles, who again, to quote Hippocrates, 'appeared to have dim vision and to be quite slack in body; he could not go near a precipice, or over a bridge, or beside even the shallowest ditch; and yet he could walk in the ditch itself. This came upon him over a period of time.'

Shakespeare refers to phobic anxiety, as do many other authors throughout history.

Queen Elizabeth I had a rose phobia, while James I became terrified at the sight of a sword.

Pascal suffered from agoraphobia, while closer to the present, Freud had a fear of travel, and Edward VII of the number thirteen. Thirteen of course is a well-known unlucky number and many people are worried when it is the thirteenth day of the month, or in some way they become involved with thirteen. Edward VII found it impossible to sit down to dinner with thirteen guests, or rather twelve guests plus himself. Obviously such a happening was avoided, but on one occasion thirteen guests did sit down to dinner, much to the king's horror and fear. Fortunately one of the ladies present was pregnant, so thirteen became fourteen and all was well.

There are very many living famous phobics, but it would not be fair to name them, and anyway the troubles of the famous are not necessarily reassuring to us common mortals. Perhaps it suffices to say that there will be many phobics among your neighbours, though the phobias they have may not in any way interfere with their lives.

Having looked at phobias, tried to explain them, and hence, hopefully, reassured the majority, this reassurance will be extended to all by describing simple forms of treatment that are available which successfully deal with phobias that are either an embarrassment, or a serious disruption to the individual's life. This is not another manifestation of the medical confidence trick, since the efficacy of the treatment suggested can be confirmed by talking to those who have lost problematic phobias. In the text actual cases of phobic anxiety will be described and the outcome of treatment reported.

The word treatment conjures up, in most people's minds, something that is done to them by someone else. This might be the giving of a medicine, surgical operation, massage, or some other technical magic provided by a professional. This is a very narrow concept of treatment and in fact we can all do a lot for ourselves and each other without depending upon 'them'. However, this is not a book which could carry the title 'How I conquered fear and came to love tranquillity'. Methods of self-help will be described, but most of us need others with whom we can share our problems and these may be professionals, friends, relatives or fellow sufferers. I hope it will be possible to cover the whole range of help and support that is available, starting with self and going on to mutual help and professional help. It will be seen that we may need to utilize the whole range, but always we have to participate even when the help is coming in part from the expert. No one has a corner in healing.

2

Fear and Anxiety

One of the problems with psychologists and psychiatrists is that they take words in normal usage and give them special or narrow meanings. Sometimes a word that describes something quite normal is made to mean something that is abnormal. For example, the word anxiety which describes a 'normal' feeling is used by psychiatrists to describe an abnormal condition, i.e. an anxiety state. Another word that tends to confuse most of us is depression. In common usage, depression is a synonym for feeling fed up, but when used by a psychiatrist means an illness which has specific symptoms and signs. A symptom is what you describe as being wrong with yourself, while a sign is something that can be seen by someone else. In the *illness* depression the victim will complain of feeling miserable, hopeless, and often guilty. He or she will also complain of having difficulty in sleeping, not being able to eat much, and suffering from loss of weight, constipation, and lethargy, together with a variety of other 'symptoms'. The observer may note a sad appearance, with perhaps a drooping of the head and shoulders, slowness in answering questions or carrying out physical actions, and evidence of loss of weight and sleeplessness. There are symptoms and signs for every emotion, be it normal or abnormal. This will be demonstrated later in relationship to fear and anxiety.

Not only do psychiatrists use words in this, perhaps, rather confusing way, but other words which are more specific to psychiatry are misunderstood and misused by those who are not in the trade. Obsession is a good example and so is phobia. Someone may be described as being obsessed with someone else, meaning that they either have strong feelings of affection for the individual, or strong feelings of revulsion. Technically an obsession is an irrational ritual, or repetitive thought. In the same way as obsession may be used to describe a dislike of someone, so may phobia. 'She has a phobia about that guy' means she does not like him, when technically it should mean that she becomes abnormally anxious and afraid when she sees, or even hears about the unfortunate individual.

It can be seen that misunderstanding the use of words in this way can not only seriously interfere with communication but, perhaps more importantly, create anxiety and ideas of illness when there is nothing really amiss. Hearing doctors talk about depression as an illness can create the belief that feeling fed up is being ill. Talk about anxiety as either a symptom of an illness, or an illness in itself, can make us unnecessarily worried about mild feelings of anxiety. Of course, this makes us more anxious with the possible danger of actually developing an anxiety state, when all that was originally wrong was being worried about a difficult boss, or a temperamental car.

Sometimes, though hopefully not often, an individual's misconception can confuse a doctor into believing that in fact something is wrong, so that instead of being reassured the patient is treated. Believing that being a little anxious is an indication of illness, the family doctor is consulted. He may prescribe a tranquillizer, and another citizen joins the vast regiment of Valium taking, 'I have trouble with my nerves', brigade. Fear and anxiety are normal emotions, sometimes they do become abnormal and that is what this book is about.

We bandy about the words normal and abnormal with gay abandon. 'That is not normal' is a common response to hearing about what someone has done, which is different to what we would have done. Each of us has our own concepts of normality. Some people think it is abnormal to consume alcohol, smoke, or to have sexual intercourse outside of marriage. Others may believe that the non-smoking, nondrinking, celibate is grossly abnormal, thus there is the individual's concept of normality. Another concept of normality is that which has been described as the ideal normal. The ideal normal could be described as that which a group of people decide is normal. A group may be a collection of religious teachers, a psychoanalyst and his disciples, a mad dictator and his henchmen, a group of politicians, a chief constable and his agents, the members of a school of philosophy, or any other group who believe they know best.

People who create standards of normality sometimes do a little good, but too often they do a lot of harm. There is a great deal of difference between establishing a code of behaviour, and deciding what is normal or abnormal. Sometimes the law of a country is taken as a definition of normality and abnormality. Thus it is abnormal to kill, steal, cheat etc., and normal to refrain from doing these things. On the whole there is a connection between law-abiding behaviour and normality within a specific society at a specific time in history, but occasionally there is no connection between a law and normal behaviour. For example today it is illegal to smoke cannabis, yet the majority of young people do this very thing at times. This leads on to a third type of normality, the statistical normal.

Normality, in a statistical sense, means what the majority do. For young people it is normal to have experienced, at least once, the effects of smoking cannabis. It is normal to masturbate because most people do. It is normal to have a sexual liaison outside of marriage, because most people do. It is also normal to feel anxious the night before an important event and be worried about death, disease and becoming pregnant. It is normal to be anxious about very many things and to experience the bodily effects

6

of being anxious. It is normal to have palpitations, sinking feelings in the abdomen, tight feelings in the chest, a tight feeling round the head etc. when something happens, or is going to happen, that makes you feel anxious. It is also normal to have one or two phobias.

FEAR

Not only is fear a very normal emotion, but it is also an essential emotion. To be totally without fear is to be in serious danger. Fear is an essential defence mechanism.

Fear is rather a complex thing, being made up of an emotional feeling and a number of bodily changes. If we come face to face with a man wildly waving a hatchet we are likely to experience the emotion we describe as fear, and at the same time our hearts will start to race, our breathing will accelerate, we may turn pale and sweat, particularly on the hands. We may experience an unpleasant sinking sensation in the stomach, a tight feeling around the chest, weakness of the muscles, trembling of the limbs and a prickling sensation in the skin as the tiny muscles that move the hairs try to make them erect. We may have a desire to micturate, defecate, or vomit, and may in fact carry out some of these natural functions. Not only is fear an emotion, it also brings with it a great variety of physical changes. These changes have been described as the 'fight or flight phenomenon', since they are the body's preparation for either of these actions. An increased heart rate pumps more blood around the body, which is diverted to the muscles, so they are ready for action. An increase in breathing ensures that more oxygen is available for the same use. Sweating makes it more difficult for us to be grabbed, while making our hair stand up would be a protective manoeuvre if we were still well covered with hair. For human beings getting our vestigial hair erect is rather a waste of time, as unfortunately are other body changes that have been described. Weakness

7

of the muscles and shaking is not much use for either fight or flight and neither are vomiting, defecating, or micturating, though I suppose these functions can rather put our adversary off. It appears that for one reason or another the body's mechanism to deal with emergencies sometimes goes amiss and this is not confined to pampered human beings. Other animals also become paralysed with fear and actually die from it.

There is a part of the nervous system described as the autonomic nervous system and it is this which comes into action when the dangerous crisis occurs. Not only do nervous impulses shoot off in all directions along this system, but hormones are released which are intended to help in the preparation for flight or fighting. The important thing is to get plenty of well oxygenated blood to the muscles of the arms and legs, diverting it from other organs of the body such as the stomach and intestines. It is this redistribution of blood that causes some of the unpleasant sensations in the abdomen, while the increased heart rate and respiratory rate cause sensations in the chest and head. All these changes, including the counter productive ones, such as muscle weakness and shakiness, are the normal responses of the organism to a frightening situation. The fact that neither fighting nor running away may be appropriate has nothing to do with the case, that is the way we are made to respond to fear. The autonomic nervous system and the adrenalin-like hormones circulating in the blood are not aware that knocking down the boss, or running out of the office are not good ways of dealing with someone enraged by our lateness. Primitive man was not obsessed with time, and here I use the word obsessed in the normal sense, nor was he worried about promotion and unemployment.

Darwin, the founder of our beliefs on evolution, examined fear in, *Expression of the Emotions in Man and Animals*. He considered that past selection had produced

8

our expressions of fear, even though the origins of this selection no longer applied to the same degree, or were of the same quality. He wrote:

> Men, during numberless generations, have endeavoured to escape from their enemies or danger by headlong flight, or by violently struggling with them; and such great exertions will have caused the heart to beat rapidly, the breathing to be hurried, the chest to heave, and the nostrils to be dilated. As these exertions have often been prolonged to the last extremity, the final result will have been utter prostration, pallor, perspiration, trembling of all the muscles, or their complete relaxation. And now, whenever the emotion of fear is strongly felt, though it may not lead to any exertion, the same results tend to reappear, through the force of inheritance and association.

Fear, of course, is not simply generated by the physical presence of a physical threat. Fear can be generated by the thought of something in the future, a voice on the telephone, a letter, an item of news, a sound, or your own thoughts. All these and many others may be normal generators of fear.

Anxiety is very like fear and in a way is a lesser version of fear. However, there are significant differences since fear is generated by a specific object or situation, while anxiety can occur for no apparent reason or be produced by situations that are not in themselves fear-provoking. The term anxiety can cover all the graduations of experience that lie between tranquillity and fear. Broadly, the mental experience and physical phenomena associated with fear are all there, with varying degrees, whenever we feel anxious.

ANXIETY
As already stated, anxiety and fear are not different

phenomena, but simply different degrees and varieties of the same thing. Being mildly anxious, or terrified by an armed gunman, appear superficially to be rather different experiences, but an examination of what happens in both cases demonstrates the high degree of similarity. Anxiety can produce a slight quickening of the heart, a slight increase in breathing, sweating, a sinking feeling in the abdomen, tightness of the chest etc. It is unlikely that anyone who is anxious will feel, or experience, all these things but some will always be present. Even in extreme fear we vary in what we feel and experience. It is not obligatory to have everything, though it is usual to have a majority of these feelings and sensations. An investigation into fear in American fighter pilots showed how we vary considerably as to which bodily change is uppermost, or appears uppermost for us. Sometimes a pounding heart is noticed, or the desire to micturate, or defecate. A cold sweat may be what is most remembered, but always there is a mental sensation of anxiety or fear.

It has been said that some of the physical changes that occur as a result of being anxious, or afraid, are not particularly helpful to us. In the same way, under certain circumstances both the sensation and the physical changes may be either unnecessary or useless. In these cases it does not necessarily mean that there is anything amiss in the sense of being abnormal. It is normal to feel anxious about an important interview, or some other significant happening. Some degree of anxiety near the time of the event does make you more alert and better prepared to deal with it, but developing anxiety the night before the event does not help one little bit. Even if it is an exam, anxiety the night before is not likely to help you prepare for it. However, feelings of anxiety on the night before an important event are so common that they are normal by any sensible definition of normality.

As previously mentioned, fear usually relates to a

specific object, or situation, and most people faced with that object, or situation, are likely to become afraid. Most of us are also likely to become anxious in certain situations, but there is a greater degree of variation. The vast majority of us will experience fear if we come face to face with a bad-tempered tiger or lion, on the other hand while most of us will have some feelings of anxiety before an examination, the degree of anxiety will vary considerably between one individual and another and there are even some who feel no anxiety at all in this situation. Some of us become anxious in situations which have very little effect on most of us. It is also possible to become anxious for no apparent reason and this can be and usually is a very worrying, and in turn, anxiety-provoking situation.

From this it can be seen that experience of anxiety can be divided up into a number of broad categories. Firstly, there is 'normal' anxiety, which occurs before an important event, or in any of the well-recognized anxiety producing situations. The degree and intensity of the anxiety vary considerably, with some of us feeling much more anxious than others when presented with a similar situation. Secondly, there is anxiety which is produced by objects or situations which are not normally anxiety productive. This is so-called phobic anxiety and is the subject of this book. Thirdly, there is what has been described as free-floating anxiety, in which the feelings and physical phenomena of anxiety occur for no apparent reason. There usually are reasons, but these are not apparent to the victim. There is also another type of anxiety, which is related to being depressed. Again there is no obvious reason for the anxiety, except the thoughts and feelings that go with depression, which may or may not have an obvious cause.

Abnormal anxiety may occur as a sudden attack, or come on more gradually. A hospital administrator I knew awoke one morning feeling mildly worried and then became almost paralysed with anxiety when he started to leave home for work. A hospital administrator's job is not an easy one, but up to this time he had dealt with all the alarm and man-made crises that were the everyday occurrences of his life. For some reason, which was never really discovered, he developed this severe anxiety which temporarily prevented him from going to work. Rest at home and informed reassurance from a physician, in whom he had complete trust, led to his rapid recovery. After a few days at home he returned to work and continued to function normally until his retirement and afterwards. One of the important problems with abnormal anxiety is that it tends to be self perpetuating. Having experienced this extremely odd sensation, we naturally become worried about it. This worry leads to anxiety and so a vicious cycle is produced of anxiety producing worry which generates anxiety which produces more worry and more anxiety. We tend not to worry about anxiety produced by well-recognized anxiety-provoking situations, but when the anxiety occurs for no apparent reason we are understandably worried. There are many ways of dealing with abnormal anxiety which range from taking a tranquillizer to experiencing a formal psychoanalysis. At a practical level, the important thing is to break the cycle. This can sometimes be done by using a tranquillizer, but relaxation is a better and safer approach. If the cycle can be broken and the anxiety disappears there does not appear to be any strong reason for deep exploration of the psyche. However, if this does not happen, or the anxiety comes on insidiously and remains with you, a good case may be made out for, at least, some exploration of your psyche and its emotional problems.

Chronic anxiety can creep up on you so that you may feel that there is something amiss without experiencing many of the symptoms that have been described. Some people appear to be chronically anxious almost from the beginning of their lives, while others develop anxiety in adolescence and later life. This less dramatic anxiety can be helped by simple remedies, such as relaxation. There are various methods and philosophies of relaxation and the method employed must depend upon the attitudes of the victim and what may be available. This is not a book primarily about anxiety, but its treatment will be considered in a later chapter.

When anxiety is associated with depression, the anxiety usually disappears when the depression has been successfully treated. There are arguments about depression and its relationship to anxiety, but these tend to cloud the issue rather than elucidate it. Anxiety is anxiety and in itself is no different, be it associated with depression or not.

Anxiety associated with specific objects, or situations, is described as phobic anxiety and we must now examine what is meant by this.

3

What is a Phobia?

All of us find certain things, or situations, mildly un-pleasant. We may dislike frogs, snakes, spiders, crowded hot oppressive streets, flat uninteresting countryside, mountains, political meetings, pseudo-Georgian houses, or anything else that can be seen, felt, heard, or smelt. Some may say that we have a phobia about the thing disliked, particularly when the dislike is irrational. You can, of course, give rational reasons for disliking all the things mentioned and anything else you find unpleasant, but this rationalization often does not stand up to close examination. For example, many people dislike spiders and claim they dislike them because they may be danger-ous, or carry diseases. There are dangerous spiders in the world, but none of them inhabit the United Kingdom, so the first explanation is unacceptable. The second ex-planation, of course, has an element of truth in it, but equally applies to many other living things which the same person may actively like. In the same way aesthetic judgements on, say, pseudo-Georgian houses hardly in-volve any degree of anxiety, but some people may actually feel mildly anxious when faced with such architectural creations.

Phobias are described as irrational fears of certain objects or situations, which correctly suggests something more than a mild irritation or distaste. However, the amount of fear or anxiety is variable, as can be seen from the following examples.

A friend of mine has the fairly common phobia about spiders. This is technically described as arachnophobia. When she sees a spider she becomes anxious with a feeling of nausea, but is able either to wait for the spider to disappear, or leave the room without giving much evidence to anyone present that she is in any way distressed. Another lady with musophobia, another common fear relating to mice, becomes paralysed with fear at the sight of a mouse, often screams in terror and on occasions has actually fainted.

Obviously any of us who has an irrational fear, however mild, can be described as having a phobia but it is the degree of fear that makes the phobia a problem. Theoretically all phobic anxiety, however mild, may be viewed as significant as far as the individual's personality is concerned, but there are dangers in becoming too concerned about mild dislikes and anxieties, since becoming concerned can make the situation worse, when in fact it may not have been of any great significance, unless we are in search of the ideally normal personality, free of all conflict, anxiety, or hang-up. It is much better to limit our concepts of phobias to those in which the individual is clearly distressed and whose life is affected to some degree by the phobia. The latter obviously depends on the type of phobia. For example, a pathological fear of snakes can be happily lived with since snakes in our society are easy to avoid. On the other hand, agoraphobia which is, broadly speaking, a fear of open spaces, can so seriously interfere with life that it becomes almost unbearable.

PHOBIAS AND OBSESSIONS

Sometimes the words phobias and obsessions are used as if they were interchangeable. This can lead to a lot of misunderstanding and confusion. Technically obsession is used to describe an irrational ritual or repetitive thought, and someone suffering from an obsessional neurosis or obsessional compulsive state is plagued with having to carry out certain rituals, or ruminations, being driven on to do these things by our ally and enemy, anxiety. An individual may have to lay out his clothes in a certain way when undressing and put them on again in a specific order when dressing. Coupled with this ritual there is often doubt, so that having followed the ritual he then believes he has made a mistake somewhere and has to repeat the whole thing again, often having to repeat it very many times. Dr Johnson had to perform a little ritualistic dance before entering a house. Having done it, then doubting if he had done it accurately, he had to repeat the whole thing. The commonest, or at least the best known obsessional ritual is that of repeatedly washing the hands, or checking if the lights have been turned off, or the door locked many many times. In the case of repeated hand washing there is a connection between obsessional rituals and phobias, since the hand washer usually has a fear of dirt or germs and hence ritualistically and repeatedly washes his hands. The following example also should demonstrate the con-nection between obsessional rituals and phobias.

A mother of three children developed a pathological fear of her children cutting themselves with broken glass. This fear then extended beyond her family to everyone else, so if she saw a piece of broken glass she had a compulsion to pick it up and put it somewhere out of harms way. Since broken glass abounds, she found it progressively more difficult to go out of the house, because she was constantly looking for pieces of broken glass, finding them, and worse still, thinking she had missed seeing them had to retrace her steps. If she travelled in a car, bus, or train, she constantly looked out of the window searching for broken glass and if she saw any she had to return to where she had seen it, search for it and remove it. Her only solution was to remain in the house and this she did until she plucked up courage to seek help. She realized how irrational her thoughts and behaviour were and, of course, started to believe that she was going mad. This fear of madness, plus a belief that she would be laughed at if she described her problem, prevented her seeking help. Once she obtained help it was possible to deal successfully with all her problems so that she could return to a normal life as a concerned mother, who still quite rightly viewed broken glass as a danger, but was able to deal with this like the rest of us.

This rather complicated case does illustrate features of both phobic anxiety and an obsessional compulsive state, but does not detract from the fact that phobias on the whole are rather different from obsessions. On the other hand, people have problems and naming these problems, though sometimes useful, should not in any way be allowed to confuse the issue. Problems can be dealt with and treated quite effectively without sticking names on them.

The lady described was afraid that she was going mad, both because of her phobic anxieties and her obsessional behaviour, and this, of course, is not uncommon. In fact many of us with a phobia or two have an additional phobia as a consequence of the others and that is lyssophobia, or fear of madness. This problem will be considered later, but here it is important to emphasize that having one or more phobias does not in any way indicate or suggest that a serious mental illness is on the way. In fact having a phobia, or two, can be looked upon as being normal. There are four million sufferers from phobic anxiety in the United Kingdom, but this number does not include 'mild' phobias that do not interfere too much with an individual's life. The vast majority of us have a 'mild' phobia. I have used the word mild in inverted commas because I am using the word to describe the impact the phobia has upon us and not necessarily its severity *per se*. Some may have a phobia about spiders, but the anxiety generated is of a low key, so like the lady mentioned earlier they are able to deal with spiders without becoming very disturbed, or revealing to others that they in fact have any fear at all. Others may become severely anxious when faced with a certain situation, but because of where they live, the work they do, and their general lifestyle, need never expose themselves to the situation, and hence have a phobia which is of no real significance to them. Very many people suffer from acrophobia, which is a fear of heights. I suffer from acrophobia, but since I am not a steeplejack, window cleaner, mountaineer, or fireman, my acrophobia has little affect upon me. If I was a fireman who had developed acrophobia the situation would be very different. I would then be suffering from a phobia in no way different to the one I have, but now seriously and possibly very dramatically interfering with my work and life. If I in my job developed nosophobia, or pathophobia, which describes fear of disease, I would be in serious difficulties, though there are doctors with this type of phobia.

From all this it can be seen that a phobia may be of great significance, or little significance, depending upon either the degree of anxiety generated, or the quality of the phobia.

Having said that most of us have a phobia of one kind or another, it does not mean that we are necessarily reassured by this information. Firstly, we may not believe it, and secondly, even if we do, we may still look upon it as evidence that there is something amiss and want an answer to the question, why? In a later chapter possible causes of phobias will be examined and discussed, but here it is sufficient to say that there are a number of theories about the causation of phobias, like there are about many other emotional disorders. Some believe that phobias are simply the results of faulty learning.

In the twenties an American psychologist, J. B. Watson, carried out a disgraceful experiment on a small child. This baby had no fear of rats, but Watson set up an experiment, in which a steel bar was struck with a hammer every time the baby saw a white rat. After a time, the baby screamed every time a rat appeared and his phobic anxiety extended to dogs, rabbits, and even a piece of cotton wool. This experiment is said to demonstrate that phobias are simply manifestations of conditioning and have no deep psychological significance whatever. On the other hand, some schools of psychiatry consider that phobic anxiety is always symbolic, with the sufferer unconsciously transferring the fear of an emotionally significant person to a more acceptable object. Someone may be very afraid of his father, but unconsciously displaces this fear on to rats or some other animal. It may be that most theoretical explanations are correct with some phobias being simply conditioned reflexes, while others have deeper and more significantly symbolic origins. Whatever the cause of our phobias there are a number of effective ways of dealing with them and it can be stated dogmatically that if you want to be free of your phobia this is always possible. This statement infers that you may not want to be rid of your phobia and some people do appear to be in this category. If, of course, the phobia is insignificant, few of us would want to spend much time, or energy, in getting rid of it, but the phobia may be of considerable significance, yet we wish to keep it.

Phobias abound and having one does not make us mad. They can be got rid of without pain or grief, but they can be kept if that is what we want.

4

Some Common Phobias

A lady of forty always visited the hairdresser on a Thursday morning. One Thursday she felt mildly anxious on her way to the hairdresser's and this feeling remained with her until, crossing the road a few blocks away from her house, she suddenly felt dizzy, extremely anxious, and sick. She managed to cross the road, but feeling faint staggered to a low garden wall, sat on it, holding her head in her hands. A passer-by, noticing her distress, helped her home. Once she had entered her house she felt much better, though still mildly anxious. By the afternoon she was back to her normal self and, remembering she needed some potatoes and tea, decided to visit her corner shop. She went out of the house, down her short garden path and into the road where she again became afraid, dizzy and faint, with palpitations, sweating and feelings of nausea. She rushed back into the house and quickly recovered again. She had developed agoraphobia, which is the commonest crippling phobia. It is not necessarily the commonest phobia, but certainly the commonest phobia to cause serious problems for the sufferer. Because agoraphobia is common, crippling, yet easy to treat, it will be considered in detail in the next chapter. There are well over two hundred named phobias, some common and others not so common. Appendix 1 lists most of them. It can be seen that every phobia can be given a Latin or Greek sounding name, which has both advantages and disadvantages. Naming phobias can be an interesting pastime, but it has a greater significance.

There is an old medical joke of a patient going to a doctor complaining of pain in the underside of the foot. The patient, as well as finding the pain unpleasant, is worried about its cause or origin, but is reassured when the doctor tells him that he has metatarsalgia which will quickly get better. Metatarsalgia, of course, means pain in a certain part of the foot but appears to categorize and explain. Thus a Latin sounding word can be reassuring, yet at the same time it can turn a problem into a disease. Fear of mice is fear of mice, but musophobia is a disease.

FEAR OF MICE AND SNAKES

Fear of mice is a very common phobia, confined very much to women. Its origins are usually in early childhood and of course there are various explanations, which will be considered later. Interestingly, it is much easier to cure phobias such as this, which appear to be there almost from birth, than those that come on later in life. Mice are still commonly found in this country and hence all the theoretical explanations of phobic reactions can apply, ranging from the view that phobias are the result of faulty learning to the symbolic significance elegantly described by Freud and other psychoanalysts. Snakes, which are another common cause of phobic anxiety, are rather different.

Few people in the United Kingdom come into contact with snakes unless they want to. Yet again, particularly among women, snake phobias are very common. Of course snakes are linked with evil as well as with healing, wisdom and rebirth. The serpent in the Garden of Eden is the best known account of the snake as a thing of evil, while the serpent on the staff of Aesculapius, the Greek God of Medicine, symbolizes healing. Real snakes come in all sizes and sources of danger. Some are completely harmless, others are poisonous but only make you slightly ill, others kill with their poisons, while pythons and boa constrictors can crush you to death. Thus there are mystical and practical reasons why we should be afraid of snakes, but of course this cannot be enough to explain phobic anxiety, since we are all exposed to the snake mythology and we are all aware of the dangers of snakes. Individuals may believe in many of the misconceptions related to this collection of reptiles and still not have a phobic anxiety.

Sometimes the origin appears to be obvious. I accidentally produced a snake phobia in a girl, which fortunately I was also able to cure. I once looked after two pythons for a friend and, in fact, became quite attached to them. A girl of my acquaintance wanted to be photographed with the two pythons entwined about her. I arranged to photograph her in the lounge of the hostel in which I was living and, having brought the two pythons down to introduce to her, discovered I had left a piece of equipment behind. I went back for it leaving her alone with my two pets, neither of whom were big enough to do much harm.

When I returned I was horrified to find the girl unconscious on the floor, with the larger python starting to wind himself around her ankles. Pythons attack by rapidly slithering towards their prey and then, raising themselves from the ground, striking the victim with their very hard head. The bigger python had done this, for some reason known only to himself. Following this disturbing episode the girl had not simply become more wary of snakes but developed full blown phobic anxiety for every type of snake. Fortunately she quickly responded to treatment, which consisted of using a simple deconditioning technique to be described later, but in spite of this she never really trusted me again.

FEAR OF SPIDERS

Spiders, like mice and snakes, are common generators of phobic anxiety, and like the other two affect women much more commonly than men. Spiders, like snakes, have mythical qualities of both good and evil. To quote W. S. Bristowe, from *The World of Spiders*; 'Sometimes she is the admitted heroine deserving of reverence, at times the recipient of men's souls after death, and at other times the villain who induces fear, abhorrence and sinister forebodings.' There is a common belief that spiders are poisonous, when in fact very few are and none of these inhabit Europe. Again, like snakes, they are credited with curative properties. They have been recommended as a cure for jaundice and fever. For jaundice, a large live house spider should be wrapped in butter and swallowed, while to cure fever a spider placed in a nutshell should be worn around the neck. In 1760 doctors were recommending the eating of spiders spread upon bread and butter in the treatment of fever. Modern medicine does not place the same value upon this maligned and admired insect.

Insects and small animals are common creators of phobias, but the best known phobias by name are agoraphobia, which has already been mentioned and claustrophobia, which is the fear of confined spaces.

CLAUSTROPHOBIA
Most of us have a tendency to claustrophobia. Reading about, or hearing of people who are trapped tends to stir up a little anxiety and there are occasions when most of us feel a little closed in upon and become anxious because of this. Being crushed in a crowd is unpleasant, but becomes much more unpleasant if the crowd is confined within a restricted space such as an underground train, a lift, or a small room. Some of us become extremely anxious and panic stricken when placed in a confined space and are the victims of claustrophobia. The phobic anxiety may be produced by any confinement, or something more specific. Some can manage travelling in the underground but are totally unable to enter a lift. Again, some people cannot enter any type of vehicle, be it a car, bus, or underground train, and of course some who are afraid of flying are in fact afraid of the confinement experienced in an aircraft.

An important thing about claustrophobia in general is being shut in, hence an individual may tolerate sitting in a tiny room provided the door is left open, but once it is closed fear descends upon him. A feeling of being shut in need not depend upon an actual physical door but can be created by darkness. You may find yourself in a confined space that has an outlet, but if darkness hides the outlet an attack of anxiety may occur.

Sometimes panic is produced by a very specific situation. I have anxiety in certain very specific situations. I am not particularly fond of confined spaces, but can usually tolerate them. For example, I do not mind being crushed into the corner of a lift, or even hiding in a trunk or box, though the latter situations do produce a slight increase in my pulse rate and a mild desire to get out. My first experience of true phobic anxiety occurred when I travelled by sleeper from London to Edinburgh. It was the first time I had travelled in a sleeper since my youth and, having climbed into a lower bunk, was extremely surprised to find that I was becoming progressively more anxious, with a pounding pulse, increased breathing, and a strong desire to leap out, open the window, and poke my head out of it. I resisted for a time but finally got out of the bunk and spent the journey walking up and down the corridor of the train. A year later I was returning from the Continent by one of the longer ferry routes and had obtained sleeping accommodation in a lower bunk. This was in a cabin with other passengers and, forgetting my previous experience, I happily climbed in the bunk and attempted to sleep. However, I was again overtaken by panic and again gave up and spent the night on deck. Examining the problem in more detail I have come to the conclusion that a bunk on a moving vehicle, together with the rhythmic sound of either wheels on rails, or a ship's engine are the necessary conditions to produce phobic anxiety in myself. It appears that this has some relationship to a very toxic illness I developed while travelling in a troopship from England to the United States when I was seventeen, though clearly there may be other explanations. It would be nice to say that I have now cured myself of this phobic anxiety, but in fact this is not the case. The situations that produce it are so specific and so easy to avoid that for one reason or another I have never developed sufficient drive to do anything about it.

My phobia does not interfere with my life, but claustrophobia can be as restricting and disturbing as agoraphobia. Being unable to use any form of transport, or enter a lift, can have serious consequences. I know a journalist who could not travel by underground and also found television studios claustrophobic. She was offered a job in television but felt she was unable to take it, in spite of the significant promotion involved. Fortunately she mentioned her problem to the right person, and at the right time, in that she had not by then turned down the offer. She was introduced to a psychologist who practised behaviourist techniques and was so quickly relieved of her phobic anxiety that she was able to accept the job. She did require a little further treatment, but now she is no longer phobic and is prospering in her profession.

There are a number of explanations of claustrophobia, ranging from some unpleasant experiences in early life to more complex psycho-dynamic causes. Many people with claustrophobia remember being shut in dark cupboards, coal cupboards, or such like, as a punishment by their parents or guardians. Joy Melville, in *Phobias and Obsessions*, mentions a Dutch girl who remembered being thrown into a coal bunker by a woman who was looking after her while her mother was ill. She said: 'I was shut in, no light, pitch black everywhere and choking in the coal dust, forgotten all day. I still shiver when I think about it. For years I could not be left alone and had nightmares galore.' This type of punishment was extremely popular at one time and I fear is still used. Not very long ago some foster parents were charged with manslaughter and ill treatment. They had in their charge a pair of twins, one of whom died, and at their trial it was revealed that they frequently confined the two boys, separately and sometimes together, in a coal hole for a day or even longer.

Another not uncommon remembered 'cause' of claustrophobia is having an anaesthetic when a child. There is a memory of the mask being clamped on the face and the feelings of suffocation and terror associated with such an outrageous way of inducing anaesthesia in anyone, particularly in a child. Again I fear this technique is still sometimes used, though never is, or has it been, necessary. There are other more pleasant and humane ways of inducing anaesthesia.

Some people appear to develop claustrophobia after a dream. One girl had a dream that she was trapped in a red plastic lift and from then on could not use any kind of lift, including, of course, more conventional metal and wood affairs. Most victims of claustrophobia remember something that could have caused the phobia, though it is always difficult to know if that is really the case. It may be that some are simply remembering their first attack of claustrophobia and not a causative agent.

AEROPHOBIA

Very many of us have fears about flying and even experienced travellers may have flickers of anxiety. However, there are many who are completely unable to fly. This may, of course, be a variation on the theme of claustrophobia and can follow an unpleasant experience when flying, or occur without the sufferer ever having flown and not be overtly related to claustrophobia. Some are panic-stricken at the very thought of flying, others have their fear triggered by taking off or landing. There is great variety in the things that we find frightening in flying. It may be the lack of control. Once in the air there is nothing you can do, except depend upon the air crew. There is no emergency cord to pull, you cannot leap out, and unless it is your own private plane you cannot make them land, go back, or do anything except complete the scheduled journey. Sometimes it is the thought of, or the actual experience of, entering cloud that is panic provoking.

Some individuals say they start thinking of disaster and view any change in engine rhythm, vibration, or even a stewardess hurrying towards the flight deck as signs that disaster is imminent.

Many air crew in the last war developed a fear of flying, but perhaps this was a more realistic approach to survival than any complex psychological reaction.

Some associate a fear of flying with a fear of heights, but in fact these are relatively different fears, though some of us who are afraid of heights are also afraid of flying. A fear of heights again applies to most of us, but some are much more afraid than others. Sometimes being only a few feet from the ground causes considerable panic, while others can climb a ladder to a reasonable height, but are terrified when they approach a cliff edge. Seeing people climbing on television, or at the cinema, can cause panic and one film in particular achieved a phenomenal success because it terrified people with its climbing scenes. Many of us with phobic fears actually obtain a kind of pleasure from experiencing them vicariously.

Many height phobics have a feeling of being drawn towards the edge when they are in a high place. Looking out of a window can bring on panic and the fear that you may be tempted to jump out of the window. There may be a feeling that you can fly, yet a dread of this. Thus there is a fear of falling, a fear of jumping, and a fear of actually flying, all of which generate panic. Some psychiatrists believe that this type of fear is not so much a fear of heights, but a fear of your own self-destructive

27

urges, so in a situation in which it is possible to jump and kill yourself, anxiety arising from this self-destructive fear is transferred to a fear of heights, being drawn to the edge, or of jumping. It may be claimed, of course, that a fear of jumping is a straightforward fear of a self-destructive urge, but in fact those who have this feeling are terrified by the thought of falling and not the dreadful injuries and death at the bottom.

Many of us have more than one phobia.

An actor in his fifties confessed that he had always had a phobia about walking across a wide bridge, or across an empty deserted square. He had been constantly afraid of having to do these things when filming, but by chance had never had to do either. He could move about normally, but had to avoid bridges, such as London Bridge and certain squares. Even a very wide street was a little anxiety-provoking. He also had a fear of heights, but only above a certain height. He was able to climb a short ladder and stand on table tops, but standing near a cliff top was impossible, as was standing on the top of a building with a low parapet. Again, he had always been afraid that he would have to work in a high place, but again fate had been kind to him. Only on one occasion did he come near to panic while working. He was doing a film in which he had to climb some steps leading out of an upper box in a theatre. He had to climb six steps, and he said that if it had been seven it would have been impossible, and if there had been too many retakes, panic would have overpowered him. In the event it was six steps and there was only a need for one take.

He did not consider that he had anything really amiss and had never even considered seeking help. As it happened he had managed to live successfully with his phobia, but obviously it had been a knife-edge situation, since an attack of severe phobic anxiety while making a film can quickly ruin a reputation, unless of course you happen to be a Hollywood star, or pop idol.

Having almost started this chapter with a fear of mice, it may be appropriate to end it with another fairly common group of phobias that relate to animals, large and small.

FEAR OF ANIMALS

We all have fears of certain animals, which are either very realistic or related to our ancestors. Civilization has brought with it many dangers and anxiety-provoking situations, but primitive life was also dangerous and provocative of anxiety. Predators were an obvious danger, but other living things took on dangerous attributes because of superstitions and all the mysteries of folklore. Phobic anxiety relating to animals may in part have its origins in these primitive fears and beliefs, but on the other hand, they may be related to actual unpleasant or frightening experiences, or a symbolic significance attached to the animal, which may be more personal than general.

Cat phobias are not uncommon and, of course, cats are associated with the supernatural, witchcraft and the devil. Witches are often portrayed as having a black cat as their familiar and were believed to be able to take on the shape of a cat. There is an old belief that cats can foretell the weather: 'when they claw at cushions wind is coming, when they wash over the ears it will rain'.

Having a cat phobia can be a considerable burden since the likelihood of coming across a cat almost anywhere is high in our society. Many cat phobics are worried by a cat's ability to jump on to tables, laps or any other place and find this jumpiness the most disturbing thing about them. On the other hand, colour is often important and many cat phobics can give a list of increasingly significant colours. The ability of cats to sit and stare is another disturbing factor mentioned by many phobics.

Fortunately desensitizing techniques usually work, though sometimes a cat phobia, like any other phobia, is simply the manifestation of a more generalized anxiety state that may require a different approach.

Rat phobias are fairly common, which is to be expected since there is an almost universal dislike of this rodent. Rats are disliked because of their connection with the spread of disease, their tendency to inhabit rather unsavoury places, and, of course, their active role in literature, films, and television. In fact, phobic fears of rats raise an interesting feature about phobic anxiety, which will be discussed later.

The most common animal phobias are of insects and birds, but mice and rats do not lag far behind.

Abnormal anxiety about all kinds of animals can be of two rather different types. There may be a fear of the animal itself, or a fear of being contaminated by it. The rat is a good example, since some of us develop phobic anxiety when we see a rat, and the cause is the rat itself. Others may not be worried by seeing a rat, but become extremely fearful if it does anything which could result in contamination. Its close proximity or the fact that it might have contaminated food, or water, generates the anxiety. As with many phobias there is some degree of truth in these fears, since rats and many other animals do spread diseases. However, phobic anxiety about being contaminated is much more than a normal fear, or distaste, and may have elements of an obsession. People who have to wash their hands frequently are described as having an obsessional compulsion to wash their hands. They may give the reason for doing this as a fear of contamination. This whole question of obsessions and phobias will be considered in a later chapter (Chapter 9).

It would not be unreasonable to state that every animal is the cause of a phobia in someone. It is equally reasonable to state that any one of us with an animal phobia can rid ourselves of the phobia if we wish and are helped to do so.

5

Agoraphobia

Literally agoraphobia means fear of the market place from the Greek, *agora*. It has been defined as the impossibility of walking through certain streets, or squares, or possibility of doing so only with resultant dread or anxiety. It can also be described either as a fear of leaving the home, or an avoidance of going out. Thus, the real cause of anxiety may be a fear of leaving the safety and security of the home, or a fear engendered by an open space, street, etc., which may be related to what happened in such a place, what might happen, or a remembered fantasy of such a situation.

Some authorities are not happy about agoraphobia being a phobia at all and suggest that panic attacks produced by the thought of going out, or being in a public place, are simply manifestations of an anxiety state, with or without depression. This will be discussed later, but regardless of differing opinions, agoraphobia, whatever its cause or place in the system of psychiatric diagnosis, is the most disabling condition of all the phobias, and can cause family upheaval, great anguish, and a serious disruption of many people's lives. It is estimated that there are at least 300,000 sufferers in this country and this is likely to be an under-estimate. It was thought that most agoraphobics were women, but in fact there is evidence to suggest that men may be as equally prone as women, but much less willing to reveal their problem to anyone because they fear they will be looked upon as 'cissys'.

To come back to the arguments about agoraphobia not being a phobia, it needs to be said that psychiatric classi-fication is in rather a confused state, particularly the classi-fication of so-called neurotic reactions. Some consider that

31

anxiety, or rather pathological anxiety, rarely occurs in the absence of depression, and that the illness depression is the central cause of anxiety in its various guises. This is an extreme view and is countered by another extreme view, which claims that anxiety is the generator of depression. Experience suggests that some of us develop abnormal degrees of anxiety, without becoming particularly depressed, while others experience attacks of depression which are associated with the symptoms of anxiety, including phobic anxiety. Again, there are others who may have little experience of anxiety, except when they leave the home and venture into 'the market place'. It is important that we do not become too confused, or too disheartened by arguments of experts and remember that problems are being solved every day, in spite of arguments about the nature and classification of these problems.

There is little doubt that there is a considerable variation in the individual's experience of agoraphobia and it is worth while looking at some of these different examples.

SOME PEOPLE WITH AGORAPHOBIA

The problem with describing actual case histories is that any attempt to provide a full and accurate account brings with it the danger of including a great deal of confusing and complicated detail. However, if the story is simplified it may be rightly claimed that consciously, or unconsciously, the narrator has forced the reality into a mould of his own creation, which distorts and destroys the truth. Long detailed case histories can be rather tedious, as well as confusing, so risking the danger of being accused of describing the world in my own image I will outline some problems which illustrate the different types of agoraphobia and hopefully compensate for simplicity by more detailed general discussion.

A lady of seventy had been housebound for forty years. During this time she had never ventured any farther than her front gate and backyard. Organizing her life within this narrow patch of earth she successfully worked as a dressmaker. At seventy she was still working with her clients bringing material of their choice to her to be made up into dresses, skirts and such like. She claimed she was never depressed but did occasionally yearn for a life outside the home, even if this only consisted of a visit to a local shop or a cup of tea in a cafe. Apparently, forty years previously she had been coming home from visiting a client, as in those days she went to the homes of customers to discuss what they wanted and carry out fittings when appropriate, and going along a street which led to the square in which she lived, she suddenly felt giddy and thought she was going to faint. Panic descended upon her and the panic increased and 'started screaming in her head'. She leaned against a wall and edged along it until she managed to get to the square. Crossing the square to her house was impossible, so she edged around the perimeter of the square, believing she would never get there, but finally arrived at her garden gate. She literally fell through the gate, crawled to her door, finally getting inside, and, to quote, 'I sobbed myself silly'. After a time she recovered and felt very much her normal self. The next day she had to visit another client, and almost forgetting the previous day's experience, set out normally but as soon as she passed through her garden gate, the panic came back in all its previous intensity. She turned and ran back into the house slamming the door. She tried a few more times during the next week with the same result, then gave up and never tried again. She was fortunately able to get all she wanted delivered and persuade her clients to come to her, giving all sorts of spurious technical reasons for wanting and expecting this.

She denied having any nervous problems or symptoms prior to this rather dramatic experience, and could think of no reason why panic had suddenly descended upon her.

With a combination of exploration, technical knowledge, or bias (whichever it is) and some imagination, it was possible to suggest a number of causes, but none could be proven.

At the age of seventy she sought help for reasons that are as hidden as the original cause of her trouble, and quickly responded to a programme of graduated excursions out of the house, assisted by support, reassurance and relaxation techniques provided by the therapist. The object of the treatment is to teach relaxation techniques and then encourage the patient to go out of the house, first for short distances, and then increasing distances, until a normal excursion is possible, without the creation of panic. In this case treatment was so quickly successful that it was likely that she had almost spontaneously recovered from her phobic anxiety before she sought help.

A man of forty had had recurrent attacks of depression since the age of twenty, having suffered four attacks in all. Each time he became depressed he found it difficult to leave his home and, as the depression worsened leaving the house became impossible. Even to think of going out brought on panic, shakiness, nausea and all the physical manifestations of fear, including palpitations, sweating, dryness of the mouth, muscular weakness and a desire to pass water. Actually going out was impossible. On each occasion treatment of his depression totally relieved his phobic anxiety, though he was always a rather nervous, worrying, over-conscientious individual, harrassed by mild anxiety and situationally created fears.

A medical student became angry when questioned by a lecturer during a lecture on the anatomy of the hand. Half controlling his anger he stormed out of the lecture and went home. He was living with his parents. The next day he felt uneasy before he left home for the medical school and felt increasingly anxious as he made his way to the nearby Underground station. On the train his anxiety increased, and after leaving the station near the medical school, he found he could not cross the wide busy road that lay between the station and the school and hospital. He became embarrassed, as well as afraid, and ran back into the Underground station, caught a train home and got a taxi for the journey between his local station and home. From then on he found it impossible to make the journey to the medical school. After a considerable time he was persuaded to seek help. It was discovered that his parents had always been intent upon him becoming a doctor and he, liking the idea, had fallen in with their plans. At school he had been more interested and able in Arts subjects than Science, but forcing himself to absorb the necessary information in mathematics, physics, chemistry and biology, had with a lot of work and increasing misgivings, succeeded in obtaining the necessary A levels to gain admission to a medical school. He found learning anatomy a nightmare and came to believe that he could not possibly pass any examination in such a subject. His parents found it difficult to support him as a student, but frequently talked of how things would be so much better when he qualified.

Family therapy and a little academic horse trading resulted in his giving up medicine and obtaining a degree in sociology, which he found more interesting than medicine and, for him, academically easier.

A woman of forty, married to a successful manufacturer, sought help for agoraphobia in the literal sense. She lived in a small market town close to London, where her husband had his factory. She developed a fear of going into the town, but was able to visit London with her husband and when there, go out shopping alone. However, even the thought of visiting a shop locally brought on palpitations, sweating, weakness, fear, and sensations of faintness. She could drive into the town, but could not then get out of her car.

Her husband, who was a rather hard go-getting individual, who would not normally be expected to have much tolerance of weakness, was extremely sympathetic towards her and her problem and expressed a great deal of anxiety about it when she was seen by a psychiatrist. She described herself as a happy outgoing individual, but did describe a number of neurotic symptoms extending back to adolescence. Because of this, fairly intensive psychotherapy was attempted, which did produce some improvement but had no effect upon her agoraphobia. Her husband developed an anxiety state, and both became involved in therapy. After a prolonged period of treatment, during which both became friends of the therapist, her husband finally revealed that his wife had been convicted of shoplifting in the town in which they lived and her agoraphobia had dated from this incident. All now appeared to be revealed, but unfortunately this did not bring with it 'a cure'. All that was possible was to accept the situation and develop a lifestyle that excluded visits to the market place. At least fears of madness were removed and there was a definite benefit from revealing to another and each other an explanation that perhaps was obvious but in varying degrees had been denied by both husband and wife.

A farm worker's wife of twenty-six suddenly became housebound one morning. She found it impossible even to go through her front or back door and because of this became anxious and depressed. Her fear of going out made life extremely difficult, since she had two young children and a husband who had to work long hours most days of the week. Various types of treatment were tried, with no success, but it was possible to develop a therapeutic relationship. After nine months of unsuccessful treatment she finally was able to explain her problem, at least in practical terms. She lived in a tiny hamlet made up of a few houses around a green, a shop and a pub. Her next-door neighbour was a young good-looking, time-on-his-hands, individual with a rather hard-working wife. They had an affair and the wife discovered what was going on. A dreadful scene had occurred and the injured wife had threatened the patient with something slightly more than murder if she poked her nose out of her house again. The patient's husband remained innocent of what was going on, so an impossible situation existed, in which the patient was afraid of going out in case she was attacked, or a row ensued which would bring enlightenment to her husband.

Rightly or wrongly, but in the event rightly, the therapist advised a little openness in the marriage and she finally told her husband the whole story. His first response was one of sadness, which soon led to acceptance, sympathy, and a practical solution. He applied for a house nearer his work and they moved out leaving his wife's agoraphobia behind. It is very unusual for any of us to solve our problems by moving elsewhere. So-called geographical cures rarely work, since we always take ourselves with us, but in this case geographical treatment worked.

An electrician developed a ritual of having to get to a certain point before an oncoming car reached that point. The point may have been the corner of the road, a lamppost, a letter-box, or many other common objects and stations to be found in streets and roads. This type of obsessional compulsive behaviour is common, particularly in children, and has its motive power in anxiety. Failure to play the game causes anxiety, as does, of course, failure to reach the point before the selected car, bus, or whatever vehicle is chosen. In his forties he suffered a mild heart attack and after this became afraid of hurrying or running. However, he still had his obsessional ritual, and the first time he went out after his heart attack he became panic-stricken. Caught in a conflict between his ritual and his fear of another heart attack the panic was overpowering. He became housebound. Perhaps it is important to emphasize here that exercise is beneficial after a heart attack, in the same way as it is prior to one, but many people do become afraid of exercise after heart attacks and distrust advice on exercise.

The electrician refused any kind of help for his combined, or related, agoraphobia and obsessional neurosis and is possibly still housebound.

These short histories illustrate how there are many variations on the theme of agoraphobia, and perhaps to a degree support the view that agoraphobia is not a discrete entity, but a symptom of many different problems. They also demonstrate some of the 'causes' of agoraphobia. Theories of causation will be considered in a later chapter, but it can be seen from what has been said that there sometimes appears to be an obvious cause for a phobia, in this case agoraphobia, while with other people there may be a hint of a cause, or no apparent explanation. The lady with a lover next door appeared to have a straightforward explanation for her agoraphobia, as did the manufacturer's wife who had done a little shoplifting. An explanation for the medical student's agoraphobia can also be easily inferred, and in fact fits exactly one theory about agoraphobia. The theory is that agoraphobia can be a subconscious safeguard against a fear, or failure. In this case it prevented him continuing his medical studies, which he felt were likely to lead to failure and disaster. One man appeared to use agoraphobia as a method of avoiding marriage, while a young married lady became agoraphobic when she developed an emotional attraction to a shop assistant.

The case of the lady worried by broken glass and afraid to go out of the house because of it, mentioned in Chapter 3, shows how agoraphobia and an obsessional neurosis can combine, intermingle, and confuse the labellers.

However, similar phobias and/or obsessions do occur in individuals in which this has not been the case. The problem with explanations of abnormal behaviour is that they can be superficial, deep, or a combination of both, and still not satisfactorily explain why one individual develops a phobia, another has recurrent attacks of depression, while a third, having experienced more traumatic things than the other two put together, fails to develop any form of neurosis, or psychosis.

Sometimes discovering a cause, or possible cause, brings with it relief and, of course, if the cause is superficial and correctable the effect can be quite dramatic. Once again our lady with the lover next door beautifully illustrates this type of cure. Unfortunately, such examples are rare and most people with agoraphobia do not get better when provided with an explanation, however convincing that explanation might be. This does not mean that treatment is of no avail. In fact agoraphobia is a fairly easy phobia to treat, using either simple behaviourist techniques, or a combination of these techniques with group therapy, and in some cases the careful use of tranquillizers. When agoraphobia is an apparent symptom of depression, or a generalized anxiety state, treatment of the depression, or the anxiety, usually cures, or at least significantly improves agoraphobia.

One general piece of advice for agoraphobics is to try and accept the resulting panic and not fight it. Trying to fight the panic emphasizes it and so intensifies it. Metaphorically lying back and accepting it makes the fear pass more easily. The fear and panic engendered by being out in the street never progresses to anything else and finally passes. Remembering and believing this puts the experience into perspective and so deals with it.

We all differ in our approach to treatment, with some of us shunning anything that does not involve seeking out the deep cause and coming to terms with whatever conflicts are revealed. Others may want a quick answer, even if that is in the shape of a tranquillizing pill, while many are happy to accept behaviourist techniques that purely aim at cure without any exploration of causation or the seeking of unconscious motives.

Many different types of treatment are, or should be, available and the individual phobic may need to shop around until a treatment matches his own expectations and inclinations. There are, of course, disadvantages to this since it may result in a dreary succession of dissatisfied failures, but few of us can be helped by people we dislike, or disagree with, so some shopping must be necessary. To do this most of us need advice and this advice may be provided by our family doctor, or one of the organizations mentioned in the Appendix. The Open Door Association is particularly concerned with agoraphobics.

Being housebound is an attractive escape from life for some, but most of us want to get out into the world and need and can receive help in escaping from our self-imposed prisons.

6

School Phobia

Most children have a dislike of going to school at some time and some detest school throughout the whole period of their schooling. This may be looked upon as one of the facts of life and any attempt to explain it a manifestation of the wishy-washy, do-gooding, it's-not-their-fault philosophy that is ruining the country. Any discussion of children's problems among a group of adults is liable to generate a great deal of emotion and expose to the outside observer a cross section of the hang-ups that afflict us. One adult may view all children as victims of parental stupidity and viciousness, helped by equally stupid and vicious institutions and public attitudes. Another will take the opposite view and, pushing original sin to the extreme, describe children as animals that need to be beaten into shape. Between these extremes there will be every graduation possible, but each affected by his or her own experiences, social class, degree of indoctrination and personal attempts to understand it all. We commonly accuse those with whom we disagree as being emotional in their arguments, while we of course, remain wholly analytical. Truth is difficult to discover, but we are all consistently wrong when we accuse others of coming to emotional conclusions and infer that our conclusions are free of so strong a creator of bias.

Allowing for our frailty, and remembering it, we need to put school phobia into perspective. A new situation tends to cause some degree of anxiety in most of us and it is not surprising that the majority of children become a little anxious and nervous about going to school at the beginning, moving to a new school, or changing classes.

However, children are remarkably adaptable and quickly lose this anxiety that is provoked by the unknown. Another cause of anxiety is that produced by fear of separation from the mother, or mother figure. This again is almost universal, but varies considerably in degree, and in the extremer version can be a cause of apparent school phobia. Thus on first going to school most children experience anxiety that has two separate origins. One is the fear of being separated from the parent, and the other the fear of the unknown. Most of us adapt quickly to this composite fear, but others fail to do so because of problems within themselves, or exposure to a traumatic experience or experiences. Then separation anxiety may be the basic problem, or it might be one of school phobia.

Disliking school, making the most of illnesses, and truanting are not necessarily evidence of a school phobia. Children can avoid or dodge school for many reasons without having phobic anxiety. Unfortunately, there is a lot of confusion about these various methods of avoiding school and this confusion can result in true phobic anxiety being denied or ignored. Interestingly, there are now many reports of teachers who feign illness to avoid going to school, play truant, and possibly develop true phobic anxiety. This should encourage us to view child school-avoiders with a little more sympathy and understanding.

TRUANTING
Truanting is a traditional pastime of children and is rarely caused by phobic anxiety, though it would be wrong and misleading to believe that no truant has a school phobia. The standard differentiation between a school phobia and truanting is that the truant does not refuse to go to school, but leaves home normally then wanders off alone, or with others, and spends the day in various ways, returning home at a time coinciding with a normal return from school. On the other hand, the victim of school

phobia is said to refuse bluntly to go to school and does not have the tendency to delinquent behaviour said to apply to the truant. In fact some children with clear phobic anxiety deal with it by truanting and some children without phobic anxiety bluntly refuse to go to school.

Truanting, said to be associated with other delinquent behaviour, happens when there has been a frequent change of school, and to children who have absent parents and inconsistent discipline in the home.

Studies of truancy, like studies of delinquency, do tend to be influenced by social background and political bias of the investigator. Some may demonstrate that truancy is related to a poor family background, while others will emphasize the poor quality of education and the boredom created by prolonged compulsory education that has little relationship to the background and expectations of the pupils. This is not the place to discuss the many possible causes of truancy, but it is worth while stating that children tend to conform, and hence if truanting is the local custom they are likely to truant. It is also worth remembering that those who blame the school are not inevitably wrong. Not only are some schools boring, dreary places, but there may also be an atmosphere of individual and institutional violence. It is very popular to complain of violence in our schools, and we live in a society which seems to be ignorant of history and convinced that violence is everywhere. While disliking violence in any form I find it hard to understand why so many people seem to imagine that we are living in a more violent age than any other, and while bemoaning this, demand more institutional violence as an answer. Accepting that there is an exaggerated preoccupation with violence at the present time, bullying by peers and authorized bullying by adults does make some children, like some teachers, truant and may be a factor in creating true phobic anxiety.

43

Some children mimic illness, or make the most of a minor complaint, to avoid going to school. Again this may be related to the nature of the school, to their relationship with other children, problems in the home, or a true school phobia whose origins, of course, can be any of the factors mentioned. A school phobia can cause actual sickness, but sickness can be used as a method of avoiding this type of sickness caused by anxiety.

SCHOOL PHOBIA

The child with a school phobia usually simply refuses to go to school. Young children will give no reason for their refusal, while older ones may explain it by saying they are afraid of being bullied, teased, undressing in front of other children, having to take a public bath or shower, having difficulty with their work or games, or the attitudes and behaviour of a teacher, or teachers.

There will be some evidence of fear and this may include some of the physical symptoms of anxiety. These include headache, nausea, vomiting, diarrhoea, abdominal pain, muscle pain, weakness and shakiness.

As already mentioned, the fear and its symptoms may occur in the home and may then subside when the child is allowed to remain at home. However, the anxiety may be delayed until the child arrives at the school. In *The Gates* by Leslie Mildiner and Bill House there is a description of anxiety coming upon one of the authors as he approached the big black iron gates of his new school. This book, which is an autobiographical novel set in the East End of London, describes beautifully both the experience of phobic anxiety and the reaction and attitudes of those involved. It creates a better understanding of this problem than any learned work, or attempts at popularizing psychiatry.

Children of any age can be afflicted with phobic anxiety about school, but most tend to develop the problem around

44

the period when they move from primary to high school, i.e. eleven to twelve years. Differing from many other phobias, school phobia is slightly more common among boys than girls.

There is usually a gradual development of the phobia, starting with a reluctance to go to school which gradually increases until there is so much anxiety that an outright refusal is the only way of dealing with it. Some do have a sudden onset, and when this happens it tends to be after a break from going to school due to holidays, the week-end, or an illness. A change in school is the commonest precipitating factor.

The following are two examples of school phobia which illustrate some of its main features.

Tommy was eleven when he really became afraid of school. His mother was a very protective lady and had hardly allowed him out of her sight until he had to start school at five. He did not like starting school and neither did his mother, but he did attend school regularly, though some days he complained of feeling unwell and was kept at home. The infant school he went to was adjacent to the primary school and he made the transition but with difficulty. For the first term he had attacks of abdominal pain, which kept him off school and his doctor considered the possibility of so-called abdominal epilepsy. He was seen by a pediatrician, who astutely assessed the situation and gave a little family guidance, which was reasonably successful. He advised the mother to sympathize with Tommy when he had his abdominal pain, but firmly encourage him to go to school. He also attempted to counsel the mother out of her over-protectiveness.

At the age of eleven Tommy had to go to the big secondary school, two miles away from his home. His mother or father took him to school every morning by car, and for the first few weeks everything appeared to be satisfactory. However, the morning he returned after the first half-term holiday he developed severe abdominal pain outside the school gates, vomited and appeared trembly, white and sweaty. His mother took him straight to her doctor, but by the time he was seen he had recovered but still felt a little shaky. He stayed at home that day and the next day again developed abdominal pain, with vomiting, trembling, sweating and pallor, but this time it occurred as he was about to get into the family car to be taken to school. Again he stayed at home, and again the next day the same thing happened. He now said openly that he would not go to school. His mother kept him at home for a period, then, becoming worried about the consequences of this action, sought medical advice. He was seen by a child psychiatrist and revealed that he had been having mild attacks of panic whenever he went to the new school, and that these had been gradually increasing both in intensity and frequency until the dramatic attack outside the school entrance.

Having carefully assessed the whole situation, a programme of treatment was undertaken involving both Tommy and his parents. This involved counselling sessions with the parents, while a desensitization programme was started with Tommy. The therapist first gained his confidence and then exposed him to increasing amounts of school. Often this consists of first showing the child a picture of the school, then taking the child to the school gates. Then into the school, and then staying with him in school for increasing periods, followed by him staying at school alone, again for increasing periods, until he is spending the whole day there. In Tommy's case it was not necessary to start with pictures, but it was necessary to start with simply going to the gates and briefly staying there on a number of occasions before actually entering the school.

Treatment was ultimately successful, though mother still remained rather over-protective.

Jane was a somewhat plump little girl and her plumpness was on the increase. When she had been at secondary school for eighteen months she started developing sore throats, headaches, earache and abdominal pain. She did not have all these symptoms at the same time, but varied them from time to time. She was frequently kept at home because of her complaint and it soon became obvious that she was afraid of school. Her mother, who was a rather strict dominant lady, decided that her daughter was simply playing up and started forcing her to school, in spite of complaints of headaches etc. This approach did not work and Jane would become panic-stricken and vomit before she even left home. Her mother tried to persevere with her forceful type of treatment, but things simply worsened, and short of carrying her into the school it was impossible to get her there. Her mother did not like the idea of seeking medical advice, but finally did discuss the problem with her family doctor. The family doctor spent a lot of time talking to Jane about school and her 'illness'. Apparently she had been exposed to a lot of teasing, verging on bullying, because of her obesity. Her doctor decided that a crash diet would solve the problem and in fact it did. Jane eagerly co-operated in losing weight, and having lost sufficient weight, returned to school without any real difficulty. The doctor did not attempt any counselling with the mother because, rightly or wrongly, he believed this would not be successful. However, he did gain her support with the diet programme, but before this he had both gained Jane's confidence and obtained her enthusiastic co-operation.

There are various views on the treatment of school phobia, which range from making the child go to school, regardless of the anxiety this produces, to a programme of psychotherapy with the child, or the child and the parents. Behaviourist methods along the lines described in the case of Tommy are often very successful, but it would appear that the combination of such a technique with psychotherapy with the family and child is most likely to produce a lasting result.

There are behaviourist arguments in favour of the hard approach, which consists of making the child go to school at all costs; however, this technique can fail, and failing makes things worse, but perhaps of equal importance is the fact that it is unkind and, I believe, de-humanizing. The hard line can solve many problems, but it can also fail, and in both success and failure its use takes a little away from the human dignity of all of us and much more from the patient.

Truanting exists and so does school phobia. To muddle them causes unnecessary misery, but to accept school phobia as a treatable illness and dismiss truanting as wickedness may help the phobic but does little for the truant. Both may be manifestations of family problems, or institutional inadequacies, stupidities, or straight-forward viciousness.

7

Social and Sexual Phobias

To experience a mild degree of anxiety when exposed to the public gaze is a very normal human reaction. Most of us, if we have to appear in public and give a speech, carry out some social ritual, or entertain (be it as host or theatrical performer), have quite significant qualms of anxiety. Most actors are shy individuals, who frequently experience agonies of panic before they appear on stage.

Burton, in *The Anatomy of Melancholy* published in 1621, clearly described both normal social anxiety and its severer forms. Describing Hippocrates, he wrote:

> Through bashfulness, suspicion and timorousness, will not be seen abroad; loves darkness as life, and cannot endure the light, or to sit in lightsome places; his hat still in his eyes he will neither see, nor be seen by his goodwill. He dare not come in company, for fear he should be misused, disgraced, overshoot himself in gesture or speech, or be sick; he thinks every man observes him.

Many people with a social phobia express a fear of other individuals and what they may think. Burton's quotation illustrates this common feature of social phobias.

It is uncommon for individuals to be so afraid of social contact that they become hermits. However, fears of specific social occasions, or social activities, are not uncommon and, while having varied forms, tend to relate to looking silly, or abnormal. Some of us are afraid of eating or drinking in front of other people. There may be a fear of becoming trembly when we try to use a knife and fork, or pick up a cup or glass. Sometimes the phobic anxiety

49

produces symptoms which cause further phobic anxiety. For example, someone who is afraid of eating in public may develop nausea, difficulty in swallowing and an expectation of vomiting. Having had this experience, a fear of being unable to eat, or vomiting in public, develops, which becomes the conscious explanation of the phobic anxiety.

A fear of blushing, shaking, or in other ways becoming conspicuous, prevents some of us from travelling by public transport, going into restaurants, theatres, or other public places, and even doing a job where others may observe us.

Nearly always the fear is that the hands or head might shake. Anxiety, of course, does produce tremor in some individuals, but most victims of this fear of shaking in public do not shake but remain anxious about the possibility. Clearly, if shaking does occur the phobic anxiety is reinforced and greater efforts are made to avoid situations in which your anxiety becomes public property. Thus, we will not eat in public in case we shake and the shaking causes the knives and forks to rattle on the plate, will not write in public since the writing may become a scrawl, and will not do work in public that will expose our shaking hands.

A woman of twenty-three started drinking excessively in the solitude of her bed-sitter. Up to the age of twenty she had lived a fairly normal life, but had always been mildly anxious and shy. She had never liked meeting new people, going to parties, or other gregarious social occasions and, perhaps because of this, had been a model pupil, gaining three good A levels and going on to study mathematics at university. During her final year, her shyness had increased and she started developing phobic anxiety about blushing, shaking, and looking odd in public. Following graduation she obtained a job with a large oil company, but gave it up after only a few weeks of work because she became progressively more nervous of doing anything in public. Thus, she could not eat in public, work in public, and even in the semi-solitude of her own office was constantly anxious in case someone came in to see her. She retreated into her own little urban cell, but even here remained chronically anxious because of a fear of visitors and her dread of blushing and shaking in front of them. Alcohol dampened down her anxiety, so she used it more and more and more until she slipped into a state in which she was either semi drunk, drunk, or asleep. She neglected herself, her flat, and her diet. Finally she was admitted to hospital with delirium tremens (D.T.s). This occurred because her neighbours became worried by her screams induced by the frightening hallucinations of this condition. The common belief that alcoholics see pink elephants, or a large white rabbit is a part of our modern mythology. Most victims of D.T.s, if they become hallucinated, see unpleasant things, such as rats, mice, snakes, insects, or other small animals of which they have some fear. This lady saw people's faces crowding in upon her, all with eyes riveted upon her face.

When she had recovered from delirium tremens she was able to describe her problem in detail and she readily accepted the suggestion that she might benefit from group therapy with others plagued by social phobias.

She entered a group made up of six other people under the direction of male and female co-leaders. The group was a structured one, which followed a laid down pattern of increased social interaction, with goals that were both pre-set and devised by the group itself. Thus, in the early stages relaxation techniques were learned and the members practised simple communication between each other, such as shaking hands while looking into each other's eyes. Progress was then made from non-verbal to verbal communication and play-acting in which social and work situations were created.

51

She responded quickly to this group technique and was soon able to go out and about and obtain a job. She in fact obtained a job in which there was not much contact with others, but while remaining a shy, mildly anxious individual, was able to live as normal a life as anyone else, and occasionally even managed to go to a party. She met a man at one of these rare parties and married him.

A not uncommon social phobia is a fear of vomiting or seeing someone else vomit. Some people with this phobia are afraid of eating out, or even at friends houses, since they become dependent upon eating foods they know from experience never upsets them. Perhaps a fear of someone else vomiting is even more crippling than a fear of vomiting yourself. One woman with this fear almost became housebound and found it very difficult to travel on any form of public transport. The sight of someone looking a little pale immediately caused her great anxiety, and if someone did actually vomit in her presence she would scream with fear. Her phobia prevented her flying because people are air sick, and this knowledge had the same effect upon her as seeing someone looking a little pale, or behaving as if they had drunk a little too much. Paleness and inebriation were looked upon as definite precursors of actually vomiting.

Social phobias, like every other phobia, affect individuals to varying degrees. Some of us may be abnormally anxious if we meet strangers, or go to social occasions where there are few people we know. This may not stop us meeting strangers, or going to social gatherings, but we may have to fortify ourselves with alcohol before this is possible. Others may manage to deal with these situations but at the expense of feeling extremely anxious, sick and worried. Others again may be so overpoweringly anxious that social contacts of this nature are impossible. Because of this variation, misunderstanding and lack of sympathy are commonplace. Some with social phobias are able to deal with them themselves, or with the aid of a friend. One lady became progressively more anxious about her hands trembling in public, or when she met someone. This extended to her work as a secretary. She decided that she would have to do something about her problem and was able to discuss it openly with her employer. He was sympathetic, and she went out of her way both to combat her own anxiety and expose herself to anxiety-provoking situations. She succeeded. Another girl became nauseated and fearful if she had to eat food in a restaurant, or even in someone else's house. She practised relaxation and ate slowly, with frequent sips of water. This approach appeared to work and she now rarely gets panic attacks.

Hearing of cases like these you may come to believe that everyone who has a social phobia could control it if they wish. This is untrue, but also has a trace of truth within it. Individuals who have severe social phobias cannot either pull themselves together, or help themselves by using the simple techniques mentioned. They can overcome their phobia, but almost always require help and support, either from professionals or self-help groups. It is too easy to fall into the trap of believing that if you can do something so can everyone else. The smug individual who has stopped smoking, but had hardly ever really smoked, is usually contemptuous of us lesser mortals still addicted to tobacco. His attitude does not help us, neither do the attitudes of the self sufficient help those with serious social phobias.

Some of us are afraid of what people may think of our appearance, the way we dress, our accent, our level of education, or our home. Again there are degrees of these fears and most of our anxieties about these sorts of things are not phobic. Perhaps it does not matter whether the anxiety is mild, or so strong that it can be described as phobic, since having this degree of self consciousness brings with it a lot of misery, and help can remove this misery, be it phobic or not. The type of group therapy already described can be extremely helpful.

SEXUAL PHOBIAS

Popular beliefs that psychiatrists are obsessed with sex and explain all human behaviour in sexual terms, can be rather inhibiting. I once knew an elderly surgeon who described psychiatrists as doctors with dirty collars and dirty minds. This erroneous belief can inhibit and make psychiatrists steer so clear of sex that they appear to have a sexual phobia themselves.

Allowing for all this it is fairly obvious that much social phobic anxiety is related to sexual anxiety. A fear of meeting people may be a fear of meeting someone of the opposite sex, and anxieties about looking foolish, ugly, or doing something unpleasant in public such as vomiting, are not uncommonly related to a fear of making a fool of yourself in front of those of the opposite sex, or, of course, the same sex, if that is your sexual orientation. Some phobics actually have a fear of being touched by someone of the opposite sex, while others describe their anxiety as being due to shyness of a sexual nature. As far as sex distribution is concerned, social phobias are only slightly more common among women than men and do not have the female bias of many other phobias, such as agoraphobia and animal phobias.

There are many reasons why the sexes may be embarrassed in each other's presence, ranging from the sexual myths and taboos of our society, which is much less enlightened sexually than many would have us believe, to single-sex education and our pseudo permissiveness. The belief that this is a sexually enlightened age, in which everybody knows everything about sexual emotions and sexual activity, prevents many young people asking questions about sex that would, rather oddly, have been easier to ask in less 'enlightened' times. Writers of agony columns comment on a number of simple sexual queries they receive from young people, who are afraid to ask their peers in case they are laughed at and dismissed as ignoramuses.

Impotence and frigidity are commonly caused by anxiety and this anxiety could reasonably be described as phobic anxiety. Fear of sex *per se*, or of sexual failure, is a guaranteed method of producing the unpleasant experience, or failure, that is feared. Once it is possible to remove the anxiety, frigidity melts and impotence is replaced by potency.

Advice about sexual problems can be found elsewhere, so all that needs to be said here is that most sexual problems are due to lack of knowledge, socially-induced inhibitions, and the mother and daughter of them all, anxiety.

8

Fears of Illness and Death

We all fear illness, pain, madness and death at some time in our lives and some of us fear these things for most of our lives. These fears are some of the disadvantages of being intelligent imaginative beings. It could be rightly said that anxiety about developing cancer, having a heart attack, or going out of your mind is being normal, since the vast majority of people have these fears at some time. Obviously many other illnesses are normally feared, but the commoner fears depend on the medical climate of the time. For example, a fear of tuberculosis was common up to the late forties and early fifties. With the dramatic decrease in the incidence of tuberculosis, due to various public health measures and the development of anti-tuberculosis drugs, this fear is now relatively uncommon, but has been replaced by a fear of heart attacks, lung cancer and madness.

Some of us develop extreme fear of specific illnesses, or become unusually concerned about our health. An abnormal degree of fear of cancer is one type of phobic anxiety, while being over anxious about health in general, with the development of all kinds of aches, pains, and other symptoms, is described technically as hypochondriasis.

In *The Anatomy of Melancholy* Burton mentioned hypo-chondriasis writing:

> Some are afraid that they shall have every fearful disease they see others have, hear of, or read, and dare not therefore hear or read of any such subjects, not of melancholy itself, lest by applying it to themselves that which they hear or read, they should aggravate and increase it.

This general anxiety about health and a fear of varying diseases can occur as a personality trait, or be closely related to some specific mental illness, such as depression, an anxiety state, or schizophrenia. Technically hypochondriasis is not viewed as an illness in itself, but as one manifestation of an underlying problem.

Phobic anxiety about illness called nosophobia is focused on a specific illness, such as cancer of the breast, lung, stomach, etc., and can occur in the absence of any other mental disorder. Nosophobia can occur as part of a depressive illness, an obsessional neurosis, or other mental disorder, but this does not apply to the majority of nosophobia victims. It can be seen that hypochondriasis and nosophobia can be confused with each other and at times be very similar. For example, if you are depressed and as a consequence become worried about your health in general, with perhaps a special anxiety about heart disease, you could be described as suffering from hypochondriasis related to depression. On the other hand, if you were particularly worried about heart disease, this could be described as a phobic anxiety about heart disease occurring against a background of depression. Perhaps this is all rather academic and irrelevant since using different names does not change the problem. Here we are concerned with phobias, and it is usually possible to decide if we have a phobia, or a diffuse anxiety about health. Going back to our original definition of phobic anxiety, a phobia is an irrational fear of a certain object, or situation, so a phobia about illness will be an irrational fear of tuberculosis, cancer of the breast etc.

FEAR OF CANCER

Anxiety about cancer is commonplace, but some of us become extremely worried about having this disease and spend a lot of our time thinking about it, looking at ourselves to find evidence of its existence, and rejecting any reassurance that we have not got it. Phobic fear of cancer is more common among women than men, tends to afflict the early middle-aged and elderly more than younger people, and is often related to a relative or friend dying from the condition.

The victims of this fear may regularly weigh themselves and interpret any loss of weight as evidence of cancer. Being told by a doctor that they do not have cancer does not usually help, since often doctors don't tell the victims of cancer that they have the disease, and doctors can be wrong anyway.

It may be thought that a thorough examination and appropriate investigations, which of course will be normal, should be sufficiently reassuring to solve the problem. This is possibly never true and can make things worse. The following example illustrates some of the features of a cancer phobia and the consequences of it being investigated.

A lady of fifty developed a fear of cancer of the stomach following the death of her husband from this disease. He had complained of indigestion for many years and finally consulted his doctor about it. He was given alkalis which helped at first, but later the pain persisted in spite of swallowing large quantities of this medicine. Various treatments were tried, including diet, other medicines, and bed rest. During this period a barium meal, which is a special type of X-ray examination, was carried out which showed some mild abnormality suggestive of an ulcer. Things worsened and finally another X-ray examination revealed the true state of affairs. He was operated upon but died two years later. Shortly after his death, his widow became convinced that she too had cancer of the stomach. She noted that she had lost weight, and looking at herself in the mirror saw evidence in her face of wasting and gauntness. She frequently examined her own abdomen and could feel a lump there. She spent most of her time worrying about having a cancer and consulted her doctor about the problem. He examined her and found that she was a little thin but otherwise healthy, however he arranged for her to have a barium meal X-ray, which was normal. She, perhaps understandably, was not convinced by all this and continued to be very anxious, and as a consequence lost a little more weight. She persuaded her doctor to send her to a specialist, who again found nothing amiss but arranged for a second barium meal X-ray. This was normal again, but she was not reassured, and in fact her phobic anxiety increased. She was then advised to consult a psychiatrist and she grudgingly accepted this advice. He discussed her problem with her in detail, and at length pointed out that there was clearly no evidence of cancer, and that she had developed a cancer phobia because of her experience with her husband. She countered his reassurance by pointing out how difficult it had been to make the right diagnosis in the case of her husband, and how he had possibly died because the diagnosis had not been made early enough. In spite of this she agreed to a series of regular psychotherapeutic sessions with the psychiatrist and was also persuaded to join a phobic group. After six months she was much less anxious, but still had fleeting fears of cancer, and these have continued to occur, but she now manages to deal with the anxiety and it does not last for long.

Physical investigations appeared to have made things worse not better, because she believed that the very fact of being investigated showed that the two doctors involved were not sure that she did not have cancer. The investigations being normal proved nothing because similar investigations had failed to reveal her husband's illness.

Sometimes cancer phobia occurs in young people, and Joy Melville describes a girl of twenty who developed a phobic fear of cancer of the breast when she was eighteen. This followed her reading an account of the symptoms of a man who had died from cancer.

This girl at first benefited considerably from being told by her doctor that her breasts were normal, but the fear came back. Treatment with tranquillizers was then tried and this was reasonably successful, but her fears tended to come back if there was any emotional disturbance caused by work, boy friends, or family.

Sometimes a cancer phobia is related to attacks of depression, disappearing when the depression is treated. Other sufferers succeed in dealing with the problem themselves, first by accepting it as an emotional problem, and then by switching their thoughts to other things when the thought of cancer pushes itself into their minds. Becoming a member of a phobic group is always helpful and, with or without psychotherapy, can cure, or if not cure significantly relieve the anxiety and its disrupting effects upon normal life.

Behaviourist techniques can also be effective.

FEAR OF VENEREAL DISEASE

A phobic fear of venereal disease, particularly syphilis, is more common among men than women and tends to affect the young and middle aged, though the elderly are not exempt. It may be related to possible exposure, but many men with syphilophobia believe they picked up the disease from eating or drinking out of utensils that someone with syphilis may have used, sleeping in a strange bed, or from the traditional lavatory seat. Syphilis, of course, cannot be picked up in this way, though the mythology persists in spite of the imagined enlightenment of the present time. Syphilophobia appears to be related to guilt feelings about sex, which are as prevalent now as they have ever been. It is surprising that syphilophobia is not more common than it apparently is, but perhaps many cases are not recognized. Many individuals free from any venereal disease visit V.D. clinics and are told they are free of infection. It is difficult to know how many of these have phobic anxiety about venereal diseases. V.D. is still a taboo subject and so anxiety about it is likely to be kept to yourself and not revealed to anyone.

I have seen men and women in their seventies and eighties with syphilophobia who only came round to discussing it with me because they had developed other mental illnesses, such as depression. Some of them had spent half their life worried sick by their fears of syphilis and when it was possible to help them sadly regretted not having sought help much earlier.

A fear of syphilis may develop into a fear of madness, since it is well known that one late consequence of syphilis is the mental disorder, general paralysis of the insane (G.P.I.).

FEAR OF MADNESS
We all have fears of madness lurking somewhere in our minds and some of us become phobic about it. Being afraid of madness quickly creates apparent evidence for the fear. Anxiety, as well as being unpleasant, affects our memories, not in a direct way, but because anxiety interferes with concentration, so information is not absorbed in the first place. Having not absorbed some information we then believe we have forgotten it, which suggests that our memory is going and madness is on the way. Fear also produces unhappy and odd thoughts, nightmares, clumsiness and general feelings of emotional unwellness. Thus a fear of madness creates apparently early symptoms of madness, which increase the anxiety, which in turn increases the intensity of the symptoms.

Talking to someone about the problem, learning to relax, and practising relaxation are great sources of relief. It is important to remember that there is a great variety of human behaviour which is well within the limits of normality. Understanding and accepting this, together with an opportunity to talk about your fears frankly in a non-critical atmosphere can do much to dispel phobic anxiety of madness.

FEAR OF FALLING

Elderly people sometimes become pathologically afraid of falling. This may occur after a fall, an attack of faintness, or some illness such as a stroke. As soon as they start to rise from a chair they may become extremely anxious, trembly, weak, and have to sit down again. The fear may not overcome them in this way, but may become intense when they have to walk across any open space inside or outside the home. Because of this their phobia may be confused with agoraphobia, and of course there can be a relationship between these two conditions. However, a fear of falling is more likely to make an old person housebound than agoraphobia in the usual sense of the word.

This problem can be an extremely serious one, since it significantly interferes with the old person's ability to cope, results in them not taking any exercise, and can force them into an institution.

Sadly it is sometimes mistaken for laziness, and I have heard both relatives and doctors accusing old people of not doing enough for themselves when the unrecognized cause was their fear of falling down if they stood up or tried to walk. One old lady said that she became terrified at even the thought of having to get out of her chair and walk across the room to her kitchen.

Old people with this problem can always be helped provided someone, who does not have to be a professional, spends sufficient time with them helping them to walk, reassuring them, and using the simple techniques of the behaviourist. The first stage is to gain their confidence and demonstrate that you understand and sympathize with their problem. Then graduate to a series of exercises starting with getting them on to their feet in a secure situation and then gradually getting them to walk increasing distances, at first well supported, then with decreasing amounts of support.

OTHER FEARS

Fears of illness can include fears of heart disease, leukaemia, dental treatment, and medical equipment such as hypodermic needles and blood pressure apparatus.

Like most fears of illness, most of us are at least a little afraid of dentists and what they do. Some of us are so terrified of dentists that we would rather suffer the agonies of toothache or lose all our teeth rather than venture in to a dentist's surgery.

With increasing propaganda about heart disease more and more people are developing phobic anxiety about the heart and circulation. Such anxieties are, of course, re-inforced by the physical manifestations of anxiety, such as an increase in heart rate, tightness in the chest, pallor, sweating, and difficulty in breathing.

One of the problems with health education is that it tends to generate anxiety. This is not an argument against it, but simply a comment on one of its unfortunate side effects. Anti-smoking campaigns do reduce the number of people who smoke, but also generate a phenomenal amount of anxiety in those that continue with their habit. In the same way, efforts to persuade us to change our ways and so prevent heart attacks tend to increase the general anxiety about this condition. Heart phobias were uncommon prior to the recent outbreak of preventative propaganda, but fortunately are often only transient affairs. When they are not transient they can cause a considerable amount of misery, but the victims can help themselves, or be helped by others. Some are able to face the problem and, deciding to deal with it, succeed by vigorously practising the technique of thinking of something else when the anxiety comes upon them. They learn relaxation, or take up yoga, or similar disciplines which involve among other things relaxation, and so develop techniques of aborting, avoiding and dealing with the underlying anxiety. Others find relief by joining other phobics in various types of group therapy, or embarking on treatment regimes advised by professionals.

Fear of hypodermic needles and injections is commonplace and we all know of someone who has fainted prior to being given an injection. A much less common phobia about medical equipment has been described, in which the victim is afraid of blood pressure machines. These types of phobia are easily treated by behaviourist methods, provided the sufferers feel they need to be treated. Obviously a pathological fear of injections is only a problem when you need an injection, and this situation may never arise. In the same way you may never have your blood pressure taken. Unfortunately, these things may happen to you in the future, however healthy you may now be. This is a good argument for obtaining help for such a phobia, but failure to seek help is understandable and is possibly a healthy approach to life. It may be sensible to prepare for the worst, but to think along these lines can also be unhealthy.

FEAR OF DEATH AND DYING
We all have fears and anxieties about death, regardless of our religious and philosophical beliefs. Age tends to bring with it a greater acceptance of the inevitability of death and most old people no longer fear death, but accept it as a friend. It is very reassuring to talk to the old about death because it helps you to realize that your present fears and misunderstandings are likely to disappear as you approach the period in your life which is close to death. Unfortunately, dying and death are one of the taboo subjects of the present and more and more young people grow up without experiencing death in others. This is obviously a great improvement on the past and no one would suggest that it is better to have brothers and sisters dying in child-

hood, as was the situation not so many years ago. By the time I was ten years old three people close to me had died. Fortunately, few ten year olds have such an experience now. Because of these welcome changes it is becoming important that we talk more freely and openly about death amongst ourselves, so that while retaining its essential mystery it does not take on the terrifying cloak of the totally unknown and unacceptable.

Severe anxiety about dying and death can afflict all ages, including a small number of the elderly. Sometimes the fear is of actually dying, but it also may be a fear of the mode of death and the pain and anguish that may be associated with certain types of dying.

Many phobics are able easily to avoid the situations or objects that create anxiety within them. Unfortunately, anxiety about disease and death cannot be avoided and may result in an individual spending a lifetime harassed by fear and anxiety, with the only relief, the very thing that is feared. Fortunately, there are now many methods of dealing with these fears and relief is always possible. The various types of treatment that will be discussed in Chapter 12 are all possible approaches, the choice depending upon the individual and his or her attitude to life and what it means.

9

Obsessive Phobias

The words obsession and obsessional have been mentioned in previous chapters and it has been pointed out that an obsessional neurosis involves a compulsion to do something or think certain thoughts. For example, some of us have to wash our hands repeatedly after the slightest contamination. Obviously hand washing is a normal part of social behaviour, but when we are afflicted with obsessional neurosis we may wash our hands three, four, or even forty or more times. Having washed once we believe we have not done it properly and again wash our hands, but again have doubts, and so the process is repeated. We, of course, realize what we are doing is irrational but attempts to stop it generate anxiety, which is often so great that we have to continue the ritual.

Obsessional rituals and ruminations are commonplace in childhood and can be rightly considered a normal phenomenon of this period of our lives. Most of us can remember some ritual carried out in childhood, such as avoiding stepping on the lines between paving stones, touching every third lamp post etc. Children, when they carry out these rituals, believe that doing them successfully will mean that they will avoid trouble that day, while failure will have the opposite result. Rituals to ward off evil are widespread throughout mankind past and present. It would appear that the continuation of these primitive beliefs into adulthood is one cause of obsessional neurosis, though clearly there must be a reason for this continuation in some of us that is the real cause. As with all such problems there are various theories, which range from behaviourists' belief in faulty learning to the psychoanalytical explanations. Most victims of obsessional neurosis have rather rigid personalities and fit a picture painted by the psychoanalyst of an individual with an over-developed punishing super ego that generates guilt and ensures a rigid conformity with the rules, laws and moral teachings. It has been said that such individuals are the mainstay of a stable society, but never do anything new, creative, exciting, or liable to result in any form of progress. This is possibly all a gross over-simplification, but obsessional behaviour and thinking exists, tends to occur more frequently in those with a rather narrow rigid personality, and sometimes causes misery and disability.

Phobias and obsessions are rather different things, but some of us do develop a mixture of both. These are usually phobias that involve contamination, or possible injury, and the lady described in a previous chapter, who had a phobia about broken glass, was a very typical example. It has been said perhaps too many times that phobias are irrational fears of objects, situations, or diseases and death. Obsessive phobias tend to be more about consequences than objects or situations, but do have a closer relationship with fears of illness and death. The lady with the glass phobia feared glass injuring others and not so much glass itself. Others may fear being contaminated by another person, or an animal, and so fear contact with a person or animal because this may lead to contamination. You may have a phobic fear of mice and become terrified at the sight of a mouse. If, however, your phobia is obsessive the sight of a mouse at a distance may not produce much fear and anxiety, but the possibility of the mouse actually touching you produces panic.

Another example of an obsessive phobia was a young married woman with a fear of knives and sharp instruments. Like a fear of contamination this was a fear more of what can be done with a sharp instrument than the instrument itself. She was afraid of harming her husband, father and mother. Many of us experience unpleasant thoughts of harming someone, or ourselves, and these thoughts may cause us considerable anxiety.

An elderly music teacher, who suffered from recurrent attacks of depression, confessed to having thoughts of murdering a child. These had occurred off and on throughout her life and in spite of never having harmed anyone, let alone a child, continued to cause her both misery and fear. She was very fond of children, yet this dreadful thought intruded upon her mind frequently and regularly, particularly when she was depressed.

It can be stated with a reasonable degree of dogmatism that those who have such thoughts never act upon them, and it is obviously important that the victims of such thoughts are aware of this and its truth demonstrated to them by those who can give convincing examples, such as the elderly music teacher. There is an exception to this truthfully reassuring statement. Some with morbid thoughts of killing themselves do attempt to do so. However, this only occurs when they become pathologically depressed. It is obviously important that those of us who do become abnormally depressed seek help as quickly as possible, since with or without morbid fears of self injury, the victim of severe depression is always in danger of harming himself.

It has been emphasized throughout this book that those of us with phobias can always help themselves, or obtain help with the assistance of others. Unfortunately, the treatment of obsessional states is a little more difficult and hence obsessive phobias are more difficult to deal with than ordinary phobias. Most people with obsessive phobias have other obsessional symptoms and usually require help with these as well as their obsessive phobia. This does not mean that nothing can be done, and in fact examples have already been given of the successful treatment of obsessive phobias. The following is another similar example.

A computer programmer had always had a fear of wetting the bed and to avoid this got up frequently during the night to empty his bladder. The frequency increased and soon he had to return to the lavatory a number of times on each occasion he got up, because he thought each time he had not passed all the urine he could have done. Having a fear of wetting the bed had not inconvenienced him very much, but repeatedly getting up in the night and then flitting backwards and forwards between bedroom and lavatory, not only seriously interfered with sleeping, but disturbed his wife who became anxious and edgy herself. Frequent rows ensued and with the break up of the marriage almost inevitable they both sought help from the Marriage Guidance Service. Following this he was advised to seek psychiatric help and grudgingly did so. The thought of seeing a psychiatrist did not appeal to him for many reasons. He felt ashamed of himself, thought the whole thing was ridiculous, feared being looked upon as mentally ill, and considered that seeing a psychiatrist had singled him out as the scapegoat of the partnership. All his fears were understandable and some of them correct.

In the event he got on well with the psychiatrist he visited and various treatments were tried, including the use of tranquillizers and sedatives, relaxation and hypnosis. All this occurred against a background of regular visits to the psychiatrist and the involvement of his wife in therapy. Because many things were tried it was difficult to assess which, if any, helped but while remaining mildly afraid of wetting the bed his obsessional rituals slowly ceased and his marriage became more normal. By this I mean it did not become a saga of tranquillity, but the normal up and down affair that marriages usually are.

Obsessive phobias are relatively uncommon, do bring with them their own problems, are difficult to handle sometimes, but some relief is always possible.

10

Some Uncommon Phobias

It would appear possible for some of us to develop a phobia about almost anything, though some of the more uncommon phobias are perhaps easier to explain than the common ones. Interestingly, phobic fear of fire is fairly rare, in spite of a universal respect for, and anxiety about, fire. During the Second World War fire was particularly feared by air crew, yet few, if any, developed phobic anxiety about fire.

Most people are rather afraid of visiting a dentist, but phobic fears of dentists are as rare as phobic fears of doctors. All this may be looked upon as confirmation of the view that phobias have a symbolic significance and are rarely a simple exaggeration of normal anxiety. Of course this is not proof, and unfortunately, proof of any cause is hard to come by. This whole problem will be discussed in more detail in the next chapter.

Since it is possible to become phobic about almost anything, only some uncommon phobias will be discussed, but this must not be taken to mean that any phobia that is not mentioned is unimportant, or beyond help. It is as easy, or as hard, to help someone with a fear of yellow lollipops as it is with a fear of mice, snakes, or birds.

Nicanor's phobic fear of girl flute players, described by Hippocrates, is obviously a rather uncommon phobia, while Sir Richard Burton, the author of *The Anatomy of Melancholy*, published in 1621, had an even rarer phobic fear. He was abnormally afraid of honey and, according to his wife, would not sit in a room with honey and knew even if it was kept in the most secret drawer, or cupboard. A well-known public figure of the present has a phobia about bath water. He becomes acutely anxious when he pulls out the bath plug and the water starts to run away. His fear is such that he either has to get someone else to let out the water, or pulls the plug out himself and then makes a mad dash out of the bathroom, with heart racing and sweat beginning to appear. Again a fear of water is understandable because of the dangers and death that water can bring with it, yet a fear of water is rare. The gentleman with a phobia about bath water has been unable to discover any cause, but a Scotswoman mentioned by Joy Melville in her book, *Phobias and Obsessions*, had a fear of water and when she remembered an incident that could explain it lost her fear. Apparently, when she was in her teens she started to become terror stricken if she unexpectedly saw a bath, basin, sink, or lavatory full to the brim with water. She later remembered an incident at the age of eighteen months, when she had turned on the hot tap of a hand basin and stood beside it until it overflowed, scalding her fairly severely. This feat of memory succeeded in removing her phobia. Unfortunately, remembering an incident, which may explain a phobia, does not usually bring with it a cure. There are few rules with phobias, as with most other emotional problems. Sometimes so-called insight works wonders, while at other times it does nothing, or even brings with it further problems.

Some rare phobias appear to have started in very early childhood. Someone with a fear of objects swinging at the end of a cord, such as lights, signs, or children's swings, apparently first became panic stricken when in her pram she saw a sign hanging by cords from the ceiling in a department store. Another individual developed an extremely strong aversion to the colour pink when quite a young child and still has it in adulthood.

Some of us develop odd phobias in later life, when it is usually possible to discover an apparent cause. For example, a lady with a fear of mud, which extends to developing attacks of panic if she sees people walking through mud on television, once slipped into a very muddy ditch and had considerable difficulty getting out.

The following examples of uncommon phobias show some of the problems they may bring with them, and the solutions that can be devised.

A woman of forty became very depressed after the sudden death of her husband. She attempted to kill herself by taking an overdose of sleeping tablets. She was seen by a psychiatrist, who was able to help her overcome her depression, but she revealed to him that she had always had severe attacks of anxiety when she saw a three-legged stool. This had been with her for as long as she could remember. She remembered screaming with terror when she first saw one as a very young child. From adolescence onward she had kept her phobia to herself, because she looked upon it as being so stupid that people would laugh at her and look upon her as silly and stupid. This had caused her considerable difficulty, since three-legged stools can, or may, be found in many places, and she had gone through life almost perpetually afraid of coming across this innocent piece of furniture. Her husband was very interested in antiques and one of his favourite pastimes was wandering around antique shops. They lived in Brighton, so there was ample opportunity for him to indulge his fancy. He and his wife were very close and he preferred her to accompany him on his rambles through the Lanes. This understandably caused her a lot of anxiety, but because she also liked being with him she had suffered while trying to show interest and pleasure.

Extensive exploration failed to reveal any explanation for the phobia, but a short course of desensitization removed it. She was pleased, but sad that this had not happened while her husband was alive.

A man of thirty-two met a girl at a party. He had drunk rather a lot and when he discovered she was a psychologist, told her about his phobia. Apparently, at the age of seven he had gone to a friend's birthday party and during the ceremony of blowing out the candles another child had slipped a live goldfish down his back. He had screamed out, causing quite a scene and spoiling his friend's moment of importance. Since then he always became anxious and sick at the sight of fish in any form. This included, of course, goldfish in bowls, tropical fish in tanks, fish on fish-mongers' slabs, fish in fish shops, and fish portrayed swimming in the sea on television, or at the cinema. He avoided visiting friends who kept fish, made detours to avoid fishmongers, and shut his eyes when there was a chance of shoals of fish moving across large or small screens. It had been possible to live a fairly normal life, but there had been many restrictions. He had lost friends because he was afraid to visit them, and could only shop in fishmonger free areas.

His new friend listened to him with both interest and sympathy and offered to help him, perhaps encouraged by his attractiveness to her. She tried deconditioning, which was partially successful. Their relationship was more successful and they married. He can just about pass a fishmongers, but is still loath to enter a house where there may be bowls or tanks of fish, and he still closes his eyes when watching things fishy on television. A wife with knowledge and understanding helps considerably.

A woman of twenty-five sought help for recurrent attacks of depression and outbursts of uncontrolled anger. She had married at the age of twenty because she was pregnant and had two further children. Her husband was extremely fond of her, but she did not feel the same about him and occasionally found him physically repulsive. She was extremely fond of her small children and coped with them reasonably successfully, in spite of living in a tenth-storey flat. However, she did occasionally lose her temper and hit them, which made her feel guilty and inadequate.

During a course of psychotherapy it became apparent that her relationship with her father was of crucial significance. He was an engineer who spent long periods abroad, and he had been absent during significant periods of her childhood. She resented this, and while having a strong affection for her father, hated and despised her mother, who had affairs with other men during her father's absence, but commandeered him when he was at home.

During treatment she mentioned a phobia she had about sharp knives and other instruments. Since the age of fifteen she had developed symptoms of panic if she saw any form of sharp instrument, including knives, scissors, razors, or shears. They had to be, or appear to be, sharp to produce this reaction. Table knives and blunt carving knives, scissors etc. caused no anxiety, but instruments for sharpening knives etc. did provoke anxiety.

A prolonged course of psychotherapy produced a significant improvement, including a decrease in her phobic anxiety. Her phobia was related to a fear of killing her father, her mother, and her husband.

These three case histories as well as illustrating some possible causes of phobias show how many victims of phobic anxiety, particularly of an uncommon variety, try to keep the problem to themselves. This is understandable but unfortunately it often causes further misery. A look at the following odd phobias that have been described should suggest to most of us that any phobia we may have is no more silly, or liable to ridicule, than any other emotional problem that may afflict mankind. There are people with fears of being beaten, bound, standing upright, of being abused, going to bed, sitting with nothing to do, churches, canal locks, dolls, dolls eyes, looking into a mirror, traffic lights, ships, buttons, home-made cakes, pips, coughing, the cold, and even knees bending the wrong way. A look at the list of phobias in the Appendix will show the range that has been named and there are many others that people have not got around to naming, though a knowledge of Latin and/or Greek would make it possible for you to name your phobia, whatever it may be, if that is what you want to do.

Having a rare phobia does not make you any different from your neighbour who has a common one. You may be afraid of thick-pile carpets, following something very unpleasant which you associate with thick-pile carpets, or perhaps thick-pile carpets have a special symbolic significance for you. On the other hand, you may be a victim of claustrophobia for similar reasons. Claustrophobia is something most of us can talk about, but a fear of thick-pile carpets is hard to mention, yet can be more disabling than claustrophobia. It is always helpful to meet others with similar problems and, however odd or strange your phobia may appear to be to you, other phobics are likely to understand, sympathize and help.

11

Causes

This is a short chapter because the causes of phobic anxiety, like the causes of many emotional disorders and mental illnesses are not really known. Theories abound, but facts are hard to come by. This may be viewed as rather a depressing state of affairs, but in reality a great deal can be done, in spite of our lack of knowledge about causation. In fact emotional disorders can be as effectively treated as 'physical' disorders. Much more is apparently known about the causation of physical disease, and, of course, this knowledge helps in devising methods of prevention, treatment, and relief. However, in spite of it being more intellectually satisfying to deal with a problem of known origin, uncertainty about the origin hardly interferes with methods of successful treatment. It must also be remembered that discovering the apparent cause of an illness is not necessarily a logical explanation of that illness. For example, it is known that certain bacteria cause certain illnesses in man, but this knowledge does not explain why one individual should develop the disease while another, equally exposed to the same organism, does not. There may, of course, be talk of differing immunity but this is only putting the argument back or forward one stage, and in the end we are left with the answer, 'we do not know'.

Having said that little is really known about the cause of phobias, it must be said that something is known about them and many victims of phobic anxiety are able to describe incidents in their lives, which would explain development of a phobia, while in others it is possible to make very intelligent guesses as to the cause.

Phobias can be divided into three main groups:

(1) Fears of specific objects, such as mice, cats, snakes etc.

(2) Fears of situations, such as being on the top of a high building, in a confined space, at school, at work, or in an aeroplane.

(3) Fears of a specific illness, of dying, or death.

Fears of specific objects can often be traced to a frightening experience in childhood or later life. Being attacked by a savage dog can create a dog phobia, while seeing a film of someone being attacked by birds can produce a bird phobia. Of course, this sort of simple explanation is never enough, since some individuals may be savagely attacked by an animal without developing phobic anxiety, while others may become phobic after a very minor brush with the offending thing. Many phobics are abnormally afraid of things that cause some degree of anxiety in most of us. For example, a dislike of snakes is almost universal, yet only a percentage of us develop phobic anxiety about snakes. Mystical beliefs about snakes and their symbolic significance are there for all of us, but only a few develop true phobic anxiety. Psychoanalysts place great emphasis on the symbolic significance of the feared object, which does make theoretical sense of a phobia but is not necessarily the truth.

Fears of situations, such as being in a confined space, can often be explained by some dramatic incident in the sufferer's past life. It is understandable that someone who as a child was put in a dark cupboard as a punishment should develop claustrophobia. But again, this form of barbaric punishment was at one time commonplace, yet every victim did not develop claustrophobia.

Social phobia and agoraphobia often have more complex apparent explanations. Agoraphobia often follows a severe shock such as the death of a parent, spouse, or very close friend, or may be associated with a serious operation, or dramatic change in a life situation. None of these happenings can relate in a simple way to the development of agoraphobia. On the other hand, many agoraphobics have had experiences that appear to explain their problem in simple terms. The lady accused of shoplifting, and the other lady with her illicit love affair, had obvious reasons for staying in the home.

Fears of illness and death also have their explanation, including the death of a close relative, or friend, from the feared illness, or close contact with a dying person of significance to the victim of a death phobia. On the other hand, many people who have had parents, or close acquaintances, die from various diseases when they were young, fail to develop phobic anxiety, and certainly in the past most of us have had someone die who is very close, yet the majority of middle-aged and elderly people do not have phobic fears of death.

There is much to be said in favour of the analysts' explanation of phobic anxiety, since it is possible to explain every individual's phobia in their terms. Analysts consider that all phobias come from repressed conflict, particularly childhood conflict, with particular reference to family relationships. The phobia is the symbol of a real fear. For example, a fear of spiders is viewed as a fear of the mother who, because of problems of sexual identification, is viewed as sexually dangerous.

Snakes, of course, are symbolic of the penis and a fear of snakes is a fear of the penis. In this way every feared object can take on unconscious symbolic significance and make sense out of an apparent senseless situation.

It can be seen that phobias can be explained at different levels, starting with the memory of a traumatic episode and ending with a symbolic significance. Perhaps there is truth in all these explanations, with different individuals being phobic because of different mechanisms. It may be thought that it is essential to ascertain the truth, or otherwise, of these theoretical explanations before anything practical can be done about dealing with the problem. As already emphasized this is not necessarily so and experience suggests that careful search and revelation do not necessarily remove the phobic anxiety, while a pragmatic approach to treatment can result in success.

Many interesting games can be played in psychiatry and these games, while being fascinating and often enjoyable, and providing an extension to our knowledge, should not be allowed to interfere with providing help when help is needed. This will be discussed more fully in the next chapter, which deals with something much more optimistic, treatment.

12

Treatment

The word treatment suggests to most of us something that is done or ordered by a doctor that will make us better. Being under treatment suggests a passive role, with you accepting what is being done to you by others. Ideas of what is and is not treatment vary considerably. Some view a prescription for tablets, or medicine, as treatment, while viewing conversation with a doctor as something else that is certainly not treatment. On the other hand, some may be very distrustful of tablets as a method of dealing with emotional problems and consider treatment as some form of psychotherapy. Perhaps the word treatment should not be used, since while having many shades of meaning, it overwhelmingly suggests something that is done to you and for you by someone else. This passive role of being a patient may be all right if you suffer from one of a small number of illnesses, but with the majority of both physical and mental disorders, the individual should and must play an active role in their 'treatment'. Psychiatric treatment, in any of its many forms, is much more likely to be effective if it is carried out as a shared effort between the therapist and the patient. When phobias are considered, it is essential that the phobic and whoever is trying to help work together as a team, solving mutually understood problems. In fact, many of us can deal with our phobias unaided, but this does not detract from the importance of seeking help, if help is necessary, and not being ashamed to seek it.

If you are troubled with a phobia and start looking around at the treatment suggested and available you may become overpowered by confusion and uncertainty. The following is a short list of possible treatments:

> Drugs, L.S.D., psychoanalysis, narcoanalysis, group therapy, occupational therapy, leucotomy, E.C.T., acupuncture, behaviour therapy, homeopathy, hypnosis, yoga, spiritual healing, and of couse, willpower.

It would be misleading to dismiss any of these treatments out of hand, except perhaps for leucotomy. We all differ in our attitudes and beliefs, and one form of therapy may be in tune with one individual, but an anathema to another. Unfortunately most of us, particularly when we are troubled, find it difficult to discover all the help that is available, and even more difficult to make a useful choice. Depending upon where we live the choice may be limited, or confusingly unlimited. Here an attempt will be made to outline a few methods that should be widely available and are reasonably effective. It must be emphasized that a most important prerequisite to successful treatment is a desire to be free of whatever phobia, or phobias, affect you. Before considering what can be done about established phobias, help at the very early stages of the development of a phobia will be considered.

NIPPING PHOBIAS IN THE BUD

Many phobias follow some traumatic experience. Usually there is an interval between a traumatic experience and the development of an associated phobia, and this delay can be capitalized upon. Obviously every traumatic experience does not produce a phobia, but the prevention of any problem, illness, or emotional reaction depends upon doing what is necessary, even if nothing is going to happen in a specific case. For example, you may never have a heart attack, but to reduce your chance of having such an unpleasant experience it is important to keep your weight down, exercise regularly, avoid cigarettes, and eat a sensible diet.

It is well known that pilots who have been involved in a crash are encouraged to fly again as quickly as possible, and the same applies to car drivers, divers, and anyone else who has had an accident while carrying out a task that they will have to carry out again and again in the future. Thus it is important that an anxiety-provoking situation be faced again as quickly as possible, preferably with the help of someone you trust who is supportive. For example, if a child is attacked by a dog it is important that the child is encouraged to meet another dog as soon as possible afterwards, in the company of a supportive adult. Such a manoeuvre should guarantee the prevention of a cynophobia (fear of dogs).

Many of us, of course, learn our phobias from our parents, or other important adults in our childhood. The mother who has a musophobia (fear of mice) is very likely to infect some of her children with the same phobic anxiety. Here it is important that the mother either faces her phobia and conquers it, or seeks help for her problem before her children are affected. This may appear to be a rather hard doctrine, but it should be fairly obvious that phobias are handed down in this way and there is a need to break the chain as soon as possible.

The best prevention of phobias is to have a secure happy childhood, with adults who encourage and guide without instilling fear, and allow you to experience frightening situations without either becoming too afraid or too foolhardy. This is an ideal prescription which rarely can be filled, and perhaps if such a situation was universal, other things would be lost. It is pleasant to think of Utopia, or rather our concepts of Utopia, but it is likely their realization would bring with it the same traps and disadvantages of the Utopia of Thomas More. Faced with real people, in real situations, there is little room for blame and condemnation, but a more general awareness by parents of what effects they may have upon their children

can only be beneficial and many phobic parents successfully hide their phobias from their children and so succeed
in preventing perpetuation.

DEALING WITH AN ESTABLISHED PHOBIA

Faced with a phobia the first thing to do is acknowledge
it for what it is and come to understand that there is
nothing shameful about being phobic, nor is there a danger
of madness, or anything else resulting. Some of us can then
deal with our phobic anxiety ourselves. The common
method is, of course, avoidance and with certain phobias it
is perhaps all that needs to be done. However, avoidance is
not usually the best method and can turn the phobia into
a crippling illness.

Many people have faced their phobias and conquered
them unaided, using a number of different ploys. Learning
to relax, as in yoga, may be the first step, followed by
exposing yourself to the phobic situation and practising
relaxation in that situation. Some have found deep breathing, or actively thinking of other things that are pleasant
helps. Anything that breaks the vicious cycle of the fear of
fear cuts phobic anxiety down to size. Simply exposing
yourself to the phobic situation and sweating it out works,
and this method is used by behaviourists under the title of
'flooding'.

Dealing with the problem by yourself can be very
satisfying and may be more appealing to you than seeking
help, but we are gregarious animals and most of us
welcome friendship and companionship. Dealing with a
phobia can be made more easy if we have a friend to help.

A lady of sixty-five, who described herself as a rather
highly-strung pianist, developed agoraphobia following
the sudden death of her husband from a coronary
thrombosis. Not only was she afraid of going out, but was
equally afraid of being alone in the house. A friend came
to live with her, which solved her problem of being alone

and afraid in the house. The friend, who had never heard of behaviourists and their methods of treatment, encouraged her to go out for increasing distances, at first accompanied and later unaccompanied. Over a period of six months she lost her agoraphobia and was able to return to the normal active life she had lived before her husband's death.

Unfortunately many of us do not have friends who are able to help in this way and may be forced to seek professional help. We should never be afraid of doing this, since a lot of expert help is available. It is usual to seek help in the first place from the family doctor, who may be able to help himself, or arrange for a consultation with someone who can. If there are difficulties at this stage it may be necessary to seek help and support from some organization, such as the Phobic Society, MIND (National Association for Mental Health), or the Open Door Association, but usually your family doctor can advise on the best help available locally.

PROFESSIONAL HELP

Professional help may be provided by the family doctor, or he may arrange for you to see a psychiatrist, or a clinical psychologist. In the recent past patients were never referred directly to clinical psychologists, but there is now an increasing tendency for family doctors to refer patients with certain problems, such as phobias, to clinical psychologists who specialize in the treatment of such conditions.

Various methods are used by professionals, which can be broadly divided into three main categories.

It is said that we are becoming a drug-taking nation and there certainly is evidence that more and more drugs are being prescribed, often with little advantage and many disadvantages. However, there are drugs which are extremely effective in the treatment of severe depression and if a phobia, or phobias, occur against a background of severe depression, the use of antidepressants can be extremely effective with the minimum of disadvantages. If we are severely depressed it may be impossible to use any of the other methods to be mentioned, so physical treatment with an antidepressant may be the only answer in the first place. Following improvement, it may then be possible to use other methods, including psychotherapy and behaviourist techniques.

It may be that in the absence of severe depression a drug approach is still used, particularly the employment of a tranquillizer such as Valium. The method might work, but carries with it the disadvantage of the patient possibly having to continue to take medication for a very long time, which cannot really be recommended. However, judicious use of anti-anxiety drugs can sometimes break the cycle of fear generating more fear, and so, while not necessarily curing the phobia make it easier to face it and deal with it.

The second broad category of treatment can be described as psychotherapy. The word psychotherapy can mean many different things, ranging from a few brief interviews with a therapist to a full psychoanalysis, which may consist of frequent hourly sessions with a therapist extending over a year or more. Psychotherapy may also be an individual, or group, treatment. In the former there is a one-to-one relationship between the patient and therapist, while in the latter, a group of patients meet together with the therapist who may play a strong directive role, or simply be a member of the group.

The idea of psychotherapy, in its various guises, is to reveal the cause of the problem and generate insight and understanding of self, with a sorting out of any hang-ups, conflicts and complexes that may be present.

Since psychotherapy has such a broad meaning it merges with a third type of therapeutic approach, which can be described as the behaviourist approach.

85

Behaviourists consider that concentrating on discovering the cause, or causes, of a phobia does not necessarily help and in fact many of us do know why we have developed a phobia, understand its symbolic significance, but still remain phobic. The behaviourist considers that a fear has been learnt and so can be unlearned. Various methods of attempting to do this are used, the actual method depending upon the leanings of the therapist and the views of the patient. Three methods are commonly used.

Desensitization

The patient is taught to relax by the therapist and during this period rapport is developed between the patient and therapist. After this has been achieved the patient, over a series of sessions, is gradually introduced to the phobic object, or situation. This may be in imagination, with the therapist asking the patient to imagine certain graduated situations. For example, in a case of agoraphobia, imagining leaving the house, then going through the door, up the path, out into the street, across the road, etc. Each step is only taken when there is little anxiety produced by the earlier step.

This treatment programme for agoraphobia may, of course, be carried out in reality and not in imagination. In the same way, a fear of an animal may be dealt with in the imagination, or in a real situation. For example, if the patient is afraid of mice he may be first introduced to a picture of a mouse, then an imitation mouse at first at a distance then close up, followed by a real mouse, at first at a distance and then at closer and closer distances. Finally he may hold a live mouse in his hand, or allow the mouse to run over his body.

Flooding

This method may appear rather fiendish, and perhaps is

one reason why behaviourists are attacked by some psychiatrists. The method consists of overexposing the individual to the phobic situation. For example, a victim of claustrophobia might be shut in a very confined space. Like desensitization, flooding can be used in the imagination, or in the real situation. Flooding does work, but the patient must fully understand what is being done and freely accept the treatment. I have a strong prejudice against this method, but this does not mean that it does not work, or is totally unacceptable to everyone to whom it is offered.

Modelling

In this treatment, as the name suggests, the therapist exposes himself to the phobic situation in the presence of the patient and then encourages the patient to imitate him. For example, if the problem was a phobic fear of spiders, the therapist would handle spiders in the patient's presence and then encourage the patient to do the same.

It can be seen that there are many ways of handling a phobia and one or other of them will appeal to most of us. Phobias can be and are cured, provided we want to be free of them and provided we look around for help and persevere with obtaining it.

In summary, the first thing to do is to accept that you have a phobia. After this it may be possible to face up to it and deal with it unaided, or helped by a friend. If this is not possible, professional advice may be sought. Whatever method is chosen it is always advantageous to obtain support in your difficulty and here the Phobic Society or the Open Door Association can be of considerable help.

Almost all of us have a phobia or two, and it is usually only chance which discriminates between having an unimportant phobia and a crippling one. To know that we are all in it together may sound rather pessimistic, but in fact it should be encouraging and this encouragement must be intensified by the knowledge that help is always possible, either from within or without, but usually by a combination of both.

Appendix I

SOME PHOBIAS AND THEIR NAMES

The list is reproduced from *Phobias and Obsessions* by Joy Melville, by kind permission of the author and George Allen & Unwin Ltd.

Air	Aerophobia
Animals	Zoophobia
Auroral lights	Auroraphobia
Bacteria	Bacteriophobia or microbiophobia
Beards	Pogonophobia
Bees	Apiphobia or melissophobia
Being afraid	Phobophobia
Being alone	Autophobia or monophobia or eremophobia
Being beaten	Rhabdophobia
Being bound	Merinthophobia
Being buried alive	Taphophobia
Being dirty	Automysophobia
Being egotistical	Autophobia
Being scratched	Amychophobia
Being stared at	Scopophobia
Birds	Ornithophobia
Blood	Hematophobia
Blushing	Ereuthophobia
Books	Bibliophobia
Cancer	Cancerophobia or carcinomatophobia

Cats	Ailurophobia or gatophobia
Certain name	Onomatophobia
Chickens	Alektorophobia
Childbirth	Tocophobia
Children	Pediophobia
China	Sinophobia
Choking	Pnigophobia
Cholera	Cholerophobia
Churches	Ecclesiaphobia
Clouds	Nephophobia
Cold	Psychrophobia or frigophobia
Colours	Chromatophobia
Corpse	Necrophobia
Crossing a bridge	Gephyrophobia
Crowds	Ochlophobia
Crystals	Crystallophobia
Dampness	Hygrophobia
Darkness	Achluophobia or nyctophobia
Dawn	Eosophobia
Daylight	Phengophobia
Death	Necrophobia or thanatophobia
Deformity	Dysmorphophobia
Demons, devils	Demonophobia
Depth	Bathophobia
Dirt	Mysophobia or rhypophobia
Disease	Nosophobia or pathophobia
Disorder	Ataxiophobia
Dogs	Cynophobia
Dolls	Pediophobia
Draught	Anemophobia

Dreams	Oneirophobia
Drink	Potophobia
Drinking	Dipsophobia
Drugs	Pharmacophobia
Duration	Chronophobia
Dust	Amathophobia
Electricity	Electrophobia
Elevated places, heights	Acrophobia
Empty rooms	Kenophobia
Enclosed space	Claustrophobia
England and things English	Anglophobia
Everything	Panophobia or panphobia
Eyes	Ommatophobia
Faeces	Coprophobia
Failure	Kakorraphiaphobia
Fatigue	Ponophobia
Feathers	Pteronophobia
Fire	Pyrophobia
Fish	Ichthyophobia
Flashes	Selaphobia
Flogging	Mastigophobia
Flood	Antlophobia
Flowers	Anthophobia
Flute	Aulophobia
Flying	Aerophobia
Fog	Homichlophobia
Food	Sitophobia or cibophobia
Foreigners	Zenophobia or xenophobia
France and things French	Gallophobia
Freedom	Eleutherophobia
Fur	Doraphobia
Gaiety	Cherophobia
Germany and things German	Germanophobia

Germs	Spermophobia
Ghosts	Phasmophobia
Glass	Crystallophobia or hyalophobia
God	Theophobia
Going to bed	Clinophobia
Grave	Taphophobia
Gravity	Barophobia
Hair	Chaetophobia
Heart disease	Cardiophobia
Heat	Thermophobia
Heaven	Ouranophobia
Heights	Acrophobia
Heredity	Patroiophobia
Home surroundings	Ecophobia or oikophobia
Home	Domatophobia
Horses	Hippophobia
Human beings	Anthropophobia
Ice, frost	Cryophobia
Ideas	Ideophobia
Illness	Nosophobia
Imperfection	Atelophobia
Infection	Mysophobia or molysmophobia
Infinity	Apeirophobia
Inoculation, injections	Trypanophobia
Insanity	Lyssophobia or maniaphobia
Insects	Entomophobia
Itching	Acarophobia or scabiophobia
Jealousy	Zelophobia
Justice	Dikephobia
Knees	Genuphobia
Lakes	Limnophobia
Leprosy	Leprophobia

Lice	Pediculophobia
Light	Photophobia or phengophobia
Lightning	Astrapophobia or keraunophobia
Machinery	Mechanophobia
Making false statements	Mythophobia
Many things	Polyphobia
Marriage	Gamophobia
Meat	Carnophobia
Men	Androphobia
Metals	Metallophobia
Meteors	Meteorophobia
Mice	Musophobia
Microbes	Bacilliphobia
Mind	Psychophobia
Mirrors	Eisoptrophobia
Missiles	Ballistophobia
Moisture	Hygrophobia
Money	Chrometophobia
Monstrosities	Teratophobia
Motion	Kinesophobia
Nakedness	Gymnophobia
Names	Nomatophobia
Needles and pins	Belonophobia
Neglect of duty	Paralipophobia
Negroes	Negrophobia
Narrowness	Anginaphobia
New	Neophobia
Night	Nyctophobia
Noise or loud talking	Phonophobia
Novelty	Cainophobia or neophobia
Odours	Osmophobia
Odours (body)	Osphresiophobia
Oneself	Autophobia
One thing	Monophobia

Open spaces	Agoraphobia, cenophobia or kenophobia
Pain	Algophobia or odynephobia
Parasites	Parasitophobia or pothiriophobia
Physical love	Erotophobia
Places	Topophobia
Pleasure	Hedonophobia
Points	Aichurophobia
Poison	Toxiphobia
Poverty	Peniaphobia
Pregnancy	Maieusiophobia
Precipices	Cremnophobia
Punishment	Poinephobia
Rabies (causing insanity)	Lyssophobia
Railways	Siderodromophobia
Rain	Ombrophobia
Responsibility	Hypegiaphobia
Reptiles	Batrachophobia
Ridicule	Katagelophobia
Rivers	Potamophobia
Robbers	Harpaxophobia
Ruin	Atephobia
Russia or things Russian	Russophobia
Rust	Iophobia
Sacred things	Hierophobia
Satan	Satanophobia
School	Scholionophobia or didaskaleinophobia
Sea	Thalassophobia
Sea swell	Cymophobia
Sex	Genophobia
Sexual intercourse	Coitophobia or cypridophobia
Shadows	Sciophobia

Sharp objects	Belonophobia
Shock	Hormephobia
Sinning	Peccatophobia
Skin	Dermatophobia
Skin diseases	Dermatosiophobia
Sitting idle	Thaasophobia
Skin of animals	Doraphobia
Sleep	Hypnophobia
Slime	Blennophobia
Smell	Olfactophobia
Smothering	Pnigerophobia
Snakes	Ophidiophobia
Snow	Chionophobia
Society	Anthropophobia
Solitude	Eremophobia
Sound	Akousticophobia
Sourness	Acerophobia
Speaking	Halophobia
Speaking aloud	Phonophobia
Speech	Lalophobia
Speed	Tachophobia
Spiders	Arachnophobia
Spirits	Demonophobia
Standing upright	Stasiphobia
Stars	Siderophobia
Stealing	Cleptophobia
Stillness	Eremophobia
Stings	Cnidophobia
Stooping	Kyphophobia
Strangers	Xenophobia
String	Linonophobia
Sun	Heliophobia
Surgical operations	Ergasiophobia
Swallowing	Phagophobia
Syphilis	Syphilophobia
Taste	Geumatophobia

Teeth	Odontophobia
Thirteen at table	Triskaidekaphobia
Thunder	Keraunophobia or tonitrophobia
Touching or being touched	Haphephobia
Travel	Hodophobia
Trees	Dendrophobia
Trembling	Tremophobia
Tuberculosis	Phthisiophobia or tuberculophobia
Uncovering the body	Gymnophobia
Vehicles	Amaxophobia or ochophobia
Venereal disease	Cypridophobia or venereophobia
Void	Kenophobia
Vomiting	Emetophobia
Walking	Basiphobia or batophobia
Wasps	Spheksophobia
Water	Hydrophobia
Weakness	Asthenophobia
Wind	Anemophobia
Women	Gynophobia
Words	Logophobia
Work	Ergasiophobia or ponophobia
Worms	Helminthophobia
Wounds, injury	Traumatophobia
Writing	Graphophobia
Young girls	Parthenophobia

Appendix 2

SOME USEFUL ORGANIZATIONS AND ADDRESSES

Voluntary Societies concerned with phobias

THE PHOBICS SOCIETY
Mrs Katherine Fisher, 4 Cheltenham Road,
Chorlton-cum Hardy, Manchester M21 1QN
Tel: 061–881 1937

For all phobics, with groups throughout the country.

THE OPEN DOOR ASSOCIATION
Mrs Mona Woodford, 447 Pensby Road,
Heswall, Wirral, Merseyside L61 9PQ

An organization for agoraphobics, with groups throughout
the country.

Voluntary Societies concerned with Mental Health

MIND (NATIONAL ASSOCIATION FOR MENTAL HEALTH)
22 Harley Street, London W1N 2ED
Tel: 01–637 0741

Voluntary Funding Organizations

PHOBIC TRUST
Mrs V. Gothard, 51 Northwood Avenue,
Purley, Surrey

Finances projects related to phobias.

Index